A Parent's Guide to

Understanding the Effects of Conflict and Divorce

Protecting Your Children from Adverse Childhood Experiences (ACEs)

Joan H. McWilliams, Esq.

A Parent's Guide to Understsanding the Effects of Conflict and Divorce
Protecting Your Children from Adverse Childhood Experiences (ACEs)
by Joan H. McWilliams, ESQ.

Published by McWilliams Mediation Group, LTD
www.McWilliamsMediation.com
303-830-0171

Books may be purchased in quantity by contacting the publisher directly:
McWilliams Mediation Group, LTD, PO Box 6216, Denver, CO 80206
or by calling 303-830-0171 or emailing joan@mcwilliamsmediation.com

Editing: Mike Daniels, Pam Gagel, Bonnie Schriner, John R. Harding, Jr. Hon. Rebecca Kourlis, Sheila Gutterman, and Jen Zelinger
Cover and Interior Design: Nick Zelinger of NZ Graphics

978-0-9768663-6-7 (paper)
978-0-9768663-7-4 (e-book)
978-0-9768663-8-1 (audio)
LCCN: 2018908258

1. Divorce 2. Parenting 3. Children 4. Conflict 5. Dissolution
6. Adverse Childhood Experiences 7. ACEs 8. Resilience 9. Resiliency

First Edition
Printed in the United States of America

Fifty percent of the net proceeds from the sale of this book will be donated to the Institute for the Advancement of the American Legal System (IAALS).

*This book is dedicated with great love to my family,
especially my grandkids: Riley, Cory and Ellie.*

TABLE OF CONTENTS

SECTION TWO:
TAKING CONTROL BEFORE, DURING
and AFTER YOUR DIVORCE

A Letter to Parents

Whether you are just thinking about getting divorced, or whether you are in the middle of a divorce, or whether you are navigating post-divorce parenting issues, you have an opportunity to lovingly help your children.

I am an attorney/mediator and have worked with over 3,000 couples during the course of my career. For many years, I have told parents that conflict hurts their kids. However, it wasn't until I discovered the Adverse Childhood Experiences Study (ACEs) that I understood that a child's exposure to unresolved conflict (including abandonment, alienation, and physical, emotional, sexual, and verbal abuse) can increase the child's risk of depression, suicidal ideation, high risk behavior, teen pregnancy and other significant mental and physical disorders. On the other hand, I have also learned that we can teach our children how to become **RESILIENT** and recover from difficulties and the negative impact of their Adverse Childhood Experiences.

It is critical for all parents to have this information. I pass it to you with the sincere hope that you and your co-parent will use it to protect your children and teach them how to be productive, happy and successful. Lawyers and judges can help. But, at the end of the day, it is you, the parents—not the judges or lawyers—who are responsible for your children. You must find ways to get through the pain of the divorce and help your children reach their full potential.

Best wishes for a successful journey.

Joan McWilliams

SECTION ONE
Understanding the Problem

1

An Overview

No one gets married to get divorced; however, people and circumstances change. Although divorce has become an everyday occurrence in modern American culture, it can have devastating effects on individuals, the economy and society; but mostly, if not done well, it can harm the children.

The challenge of divorce is finding paths that allow you, as parents, to define new roles, step into new lives and raise your children. Some people do this with thoughtfulness and grace, and others do not.

I am an attorney, mediator, mother and grandmother, and I have worked with divorcing couples for over thirty years. I've found that people who are committed to achieving amicable divorces make my job easy, and they make their lives much easier. They avoid costly litigation and the inevitable scarring that unresolved anger creates. They avoid the psychological damage caused by disputes. Most importantly, they keep their children out of the fray and allow their kids to thrive.

Couples who are experiencing conflict are more challenging and much more heartbreaking. They often exploit our adversarial legal system that inherently, by its design, supports their anger. Each must prove they are right and that the other parent is wrong. Each strives to prove that they are the "better parent." Often, they must wait a year or longer for their case to be heard by a judge, only to be given mere hours to present their facts and arguments. Their "day in court" can be elusive, but they may spend literally hundreds of thousands of dollars on lawyers, experts and mental health professionals in an attempt to beat the other parent—the parent of their very own children. The children's best interests are almost always lost in the fight, and the judge (who knows neither the parents nor the children) makes decisions that affect the kids and the parents for the rest of their lives.

At the end of the day, the judge and the professionals go home, and the parents are left to raise their children in the hostile environments they have created. In many cases, the parents literally destroy all hope they may have had for giving their children a happy childhood and a productive life. The damage can be irreparable.

When I repeatedly see parents who, by their behavior, harm their children, I often wonder how we have failed to teach them that their anger and aggressive behavior in the presence of their kids can scar their children forever.

How have we failed to help parents understand that verbal abuse can be as devastating as physical abuse?

How have we failed to teach parents about the devastating effects of alienation and abandonment?

How have we failed to create a legal system that supports families and discourages fighting?

How have we tolerated statements like, "I'll see you in court," or "You'll never see the children again"?

How have we allowed these and similar comments to become ingrained in our psyches?

The answers are all but irrelevant because the result is the same: We are hurting our children.

> *This is a public health crisis. More than one-half of all divorces involve children under the age of eighteen.[i] Many of them witness violence, anger, verbal abuse, alienation, abandonment and unrelenting stress. Many are irreversibly scarred.*

Throughout my practice, I have told parents that conflict hurts kids. While this seems obvious, it is easily forgotten when winning and survival take over. We now, however, have shocking proof that unresolved parental conflict (even low conflict) can damage children, and that damage can affect them for the rest of their lives:

- We know that **Adverse Childhood Experiences (ACEs)** can create toxic stress in your children. ACEs include, among other things:

  o experiencing verbal, emotional, physical or sexual abuse

  o experiencing physical or emotional neglect

  o being unloved or unprotected;

  o losing a biological parent through divorce, abandonment or other reasons o living with an alcoholic or drug-addicted parent

o living with a depressed, mentally ill or incarcerated person

o witnessing violence against one's mother.

Each of these damaging experiences increases a child's risk of depression, suicide, high-risk behavior, teen pregnancy, substance abuse, and mental and physical disorders.[ii]

- We know that verbal abuse actually affects a child's brain development and is considered to be an ACE.[iii] This is information that should be required learning for every parent.

- We know that, without help and support, children may never recover from being abandoned, or perceiving themselves to be abandoned, by a parent or being turned against one parent by the alienating behavior of the other.

- We know that sudden emotional stress can result in a phenomenon known as "broken heart syndrome," which can cause physical changes and even death.[iv]

- We know that children are particularly susceptible to real or perceived societal conflict, such as actual or threatened violence or virtual violence that comes into your children's lives through TV, the internet, video games, and explicit recordings. Cyberbullying, violence, and pornography are all available to your children if they have unrestricted access to a smartphone or tablet. Societal conflict, while not necessarily connected to divorce, adds another layer to the original ACEs and enhances the devastating chaos.

However ... and this is the **GOOD NEWS**, we also know that children can develop *RESILIENCE*, which is the ability to recover from difficulties and the negative impact of Adverse Childhood Experiences.

You may be acquainted with people who carry the burden of ACEs they experienced as children. I know that whenever I am in a group and someone discovers that I am a divorce mediator, that person invariably wants to tell me their story. I have also done many presentations with adult children of divorce in which they share their experiences. The stories are always poignant, as they inevitably harken back to childhood episodes that have never left the storyteller.

Jacqueline, for example, rarely participates in a conversation without mentioning her father. Jacqueline is a bright and energetic woman. However, in most discussions, she will inevitably say, "My dad loved me ... oh, how my dad loved me." Jacqueline was rejected and basically abandoned by her father when he remarried after her parent's divorce. She was sixteen and didn't see him for most of her adult life. Jacqueline is eighty-two-years old and still carries the pain of her father's abandonment.

Evelyn, a thirty-year-old businesswoman, physically shakes when she experiences conflict. She has come to realize that her tremors started as a young child, sitting on the stairs with her brother, listening to their parents fight and feeling desperately afraid that they would hurt each other or hurt one of them. Today, it is difficult for her to enter into or maintain a committed relationship.

Children of divorce, at every age, tell us how the turmoil of their parent's divorce affected and continues to affect their emotional and physical health, their school and work performance, and their ability to enter into friendships and intimate relationships. In light of this, doesn't it make sense to change the way we approach divorce, to speak as a community and say that unresolved parental conflict in the presence of children is unacceptable? Doesn't it make sense to insist that parents work together to protect their children? And doesn't it make sense for us to expect parents to take back their power, anticipate the perils of the legal system and design their own, unique Post-Divorce Family?

For the benefit of the children, we, as individuals, as parents and as communities must:

- Recognize the potential harm unresolved parental conflict and Adverse Childhood Experiences can do to children, and do our best to remove it from their experience.

- Recognize the potential harm that societal conflict can have on children and do our best to protect them.

- Listen to and hear the voices of the children, and help them become **Resilient.**

- Support and use trauma-informed child and family service systems in which professionals are trained to recognize and respond to the impact of traumatic stress in children and their caregivers;

- Demand that the first question divorce lawyers, therapists, mediators and judges ask of divorce clients and litigants will be, "How can we protect the children?"

- Speak as a community to reject damaging parental misbehavior, in the same way we reject public smoking and drunk driving.

It's your turn.

The courts valiantly try to address the effects of parental conflict on children, but the legal system can only do so much. Ultimately, it is you, the parents, who must take responsibility. You must anticipate problems and make agreements with your co-parent, with yourself, and with the community to protect all children, especially your own. You can make the important difference. As a result of your efforts, other families, our schools, our courts, our workplaces and our nation will benefit.

That's what this book is about.

- In the first section, you will learn about toxic stress, Adverse Childhood Experiences (ACEs), and how

ACEs can actually change the course of your children's lives. But keep reading … in the first section, you will also learn how to reduce the effects of ACEs and toxic stress and help your children develop **Resilience**.

- In the second section, you will learn how to create action plans for you and your co-parent. These plans will help your children become more resilient and assist you in coping with your divorce. You will also learn how you and your friends can make a difference in your community.

- In the third section, you will learn easy cues that you can mentally review and consider in times of stress.

You can change the way you approach divorce—before, during and after your separation. *It's up to you.* You can create space for your children to have a healthy path to adulthood, *and* you can create space for yourself to move on in your life. But to do so, you *must* start planning and insisting on the way you and your co-parent will handle your divorce or, if the other parent is uncooperative, the way *you* will handle the divorce, for your children's sake.

2

Conflict and Stress— Good and Bad

Divorce is a breathtaking process that can toss you onto an emotional roller coaster and throw you upside down and sideways. Divorce can be lonely, and definitely scary. It can crush your "happily ever after" dream and leave you with unremitting sadness and grief.

But what about your children?

Their dream of an intact family will be gone. They may lose their house, their friends and their school.

Will they be destroyed?

No ... not if you provide an experience for them that promotes their growth and helps them move confidently into adulthood. For most families, that is totally within the realm of possibility, but first, you must understand conflict, stress and the damage it can do to your children.

Conflict and Stress—Positive, Tolerable and Toxic

There are very few parents who can get through the emotions of a divorce without conflict. It can be loud, accusatory and unremitting, or it can be subtle and scarring. In the pain of the moment, couples do not care who witnesses their anger. Unfortunately, it is often the children. As a result, the children experience stress.

Positive Stress

There are different types of stress, each of which lead to different outcomes.[v] The first type of stress is referred to as "positive stress." It is short-lived and occurs, for example, when a child meets a new person or deals with frustration. It occurs in the context of stable and supportive relationships and is important for a child's healthy development.

When you go through a divorce, you and your children will, on some level, experience both conflict and stress. The conflict may be minimal, especially if the divorce is mutual and there are no outside factors (such as new significant others) that contribute to the problem. There will, however, always be stress. It may be emotional or financial. It may be caused by a mandatory lifestyle adjustment and acceptance of new ideas, rules, restrictions or living in two homes.

If both parents are cooperative and do not suffer from mental, physical, alcohol/drug abuse or financial problems, and if each can accept the involvement of the other parent in their children's lives, the divorce can be sufficiently amicable. The children will have reliable parents to provide the consistency and stability that they need. This is an example of a low conflict/positive stress divorce. It is likely to have a good outcome for the children. Low conflict divorces are unusual, however, because divorce almost always creates disagreements that affect both parents and children.

Tolerable Stress

The second type of stress is known as "tolerable stress," which is associated with events that are large enough to disrupt your child's brain development, but are relieved by supportive relationships.[vi] These experiences include the death of a loved one, divorce of one's parents, a natural disaster or an event such as 9-11.

Tolerable stress can have long-term effects if the children don't have a trusted and supportive adult who will protect them by reducing their sense of being overwhelmed. In other words, someone, such as a parent, therapist or religious leader, who can "turn down" their stress response system (i.e., heart rate, blood pressure and stress hormones).

It's important to recognize the critical role that parents play in the tolerable stress divorce. Stress is present, and it may be significant. But the children are not caught in the middle, and they have at least one parent who can protect them. It is very helpful if the children see that their parents can resolve the conflict. If both parents are involved in the parenting and actively involved with their children, both parents will work cooperatively to help the children cope.

Toxic Stress

Finally, we observe the third kind of stress: toxic stress. Toxic stress "can occur when a child experiences strong, frequent and/or prolonged adversity—such as physical or emotional abuse, chronic neglect, caregiver substance abuse or mental illness, exposure to violence, and/or the accumulated burdens of family economic hardship—without adequate adult support."[vii] In these situations, a child's brain development can actually be altered. Toxic stress in early childhood can result in a lifetime of greater susceptibility to health problems such as heart disease, diabetes, substance abuse and depression.[viii]

Most children will experience positive stress and tolerable stress, and they are likely to get through the experiences just fine, particularly if they have loving and stable adults as guides. Toxic stress is different. As described below, it is harmful and can have lifelong consequences.

The best way to handle toxic stress is to prevent or avoid it. Absent that, it is important to recognize when you are exposing your children to toxic stress and to create an environment in which your children learn to manage the stress and develop healthy relationships. You, the parents, must protect them and teach them to be resilient.

3

Adverse Childhood Experiences (ACEs)

*A*lec and Melinda entered the courthouse through separate doors. They inadvertently met in the lobby and were forced to stand in line together to go through the metal detector. They glared at each other, and any anger that might have subsided from their divorce ten years earlier was rekindled and ignited.

Time had not been kind to them. Alec was nearly fifty-five and showed the effects of years of compulsive work and enthusiastic partying. Balding and paunchy, he didn't wear the vicissitudes of life with any degree of grace.

Melinda was fifty, but also looked tired and older than her years. She had gone through the money she received in the divorce. She had completed graduate school and had a good job as a school administrator, but she exuded anger and unhappiness. It was as if she had allowed life to deal her a harsh blow from which she might never fully recover.

Alec and Melinda had a son, Tim, who was an unexpected but welcome addition to their family. He was a healthy baby and brought them great joy. However, with time, Alec and

Melinda were unable to overcome the pressures of their lives and the distance that had crept between them. Their fighting became more intense, as did the extramarital affairs. Although they tried to shield Tim from their disagreements, they were not successful. Tim was witness to their verbal and physical abuse. On many occasions, their son caught the brunt of their anger and frustration.

Their divorce was no different from their marriage. They had protracted court battles. They fought whenever they saw each other—even when Tim was present. They fought in court and continued to fight, even after the judge banged the gavel and declared them to be legally divorced.

Their fighting continued outside the courtroom and into their co-parenting life. They argued over parenting time, Tim's activities and his schoolwork. They argued during his soccer games and other events, humiliating Tim in front of his friends, teachers and coaches.

And they didn't just argue with each other. They often turned their anger towards Tim. It was not unusual for one or the other of them to swear at him, hit him and denigrate him to the point that he felt worthless.

Once Tim entered high school, he befriended other boys who had become estranged from their families. One thing followed another: alcohol, smoking, marijuana and finally methamphetamine. Tim suffered from depression. He self-medicated on drugs and began stealing to support his habits. He was arrested on several occasions, but his parents were always able to get lawyers for him. He managed to beat the charges—except for the last time when he broke into a house with a gun ... armed robbery ... and that was the end of the line.

Alec and Melinda did not speak as they traveled the long corridor to the courtroom where Tim was to be sentenced. Finally, Melinda broke the silence, hurling a vitriolic statement at Alec about his girlfriend. Alec quickly shot back, cursing Melinda's infidelity. And, with that, they instantly regressed to the behavior they experienced throughout the marriage: loud and vicious arguing in the presence of their son.

They were still arguing when they entered the courtroom. They were still arguing when their son, Tim, was brought into the courtroom, wearing an orange jumpsuit and shackles. Tim looked at his parents and tried to make eye contact, but they were glaring at each other and didn't notice his pleading glances.

As the judge announced the sentence, Tim again turned to his parents, with tears in his eyes. They didn't respond but maintained their hateful exchanges. As the sheriff's deputies led him out, Tim gave his parents one last tearful glance, but they weren't watching.

This outcome is sad but predictable. Eighty percent of the kids entering the juvenile justice system in a large metropolitan district court near Denver, Colorado, for example, experienced their parent's high-conflict divorce or abandonment.[ix]

Adverse Childhood Experiences Study

Mental health professionals invariably agree: When children witness or are put in the middle of unresolved parental conflict, it increases the likelihood that they will have adjustment issues after the divorce.[x] However, based on a progression of studies that began in 1995 and continue to the present, we have a way to predict precisely how conflict actually affects children. The answer is found in the Adverse Childhood Experiences Study.[xi]

In this 1997 study, Robert Anda, MD, formerly with the US Centers for Disease Control and Prevention, and Vincent Felitti, MD, formerly with the Kaiser Permanente Medical Care Program in San Diego, California, collaborated to evaluate the correlation between childhood traumatic stress and adult physical and emotional difficulties. This became known as the Adverse Childhood Experience (ACEs) Study and included more than 17,000 adults (a very large number for this kind of research) who were enrolled in the Kaiser HMO in San Diego, California.

Participants were given a questionnaire addressing ten Adverse Childhood Experiences (ACEs) that they may have experienced during childhood. The questionnaire that Drs. Anda and Felitti gave their volunteers was remarkably simple. It included the following questions:

While you were growing up, during your first eighteen years of life:

1. Did a parent or other adult in the household **often** …
   Swear at you, insult you, put you down or humiliate you?

   or

Act in a way that made you afraid that you might be physically hurt?

Yes No   If yes, enter 1 _____

2. Did a parent or other adult in the household **often** ...
Push, grab, slap or throw something at you?
   or
Ever hit you so hard that you had marks or were injured?

Yes No   If yes, enter 1 _____

3. Did an adult or person at least five years older than you **ever** ...
Touch or fondle you or have you touch their body in a sexual way?
   or
Attempt to or actually have oral, anal or vaginal sex with you?

Yes No   If yes, enter 1 _____

4. Did you **often** feel that ...
No one in your family loved you or thought you were important or special?
   or
Your family didn't look out for each other, feel close to each other, or support each other?

Yes No   If yes, enter 1 _____

5. Did you **often** feel that …
   You didn't have enough to eat, had to wear dirty clothes, and had no one to protect you?
   > **or**

   Your parents were too drunk or high to take care of you or take you to the doctor if you needed it?
   > Yes No   If yes, enter 1 _____

6. Was a biological parent ever lost to you through divorce, abandonment or other reason?
   > Yes No   If yes, enter 1_____

7. Was your mother or stepmother:
   Often pushed, grabbed, slapped, or had something thrown at her?
   > **or**

   Sometimes or often kicked, bitten, hit with a fist, or hit with something hard?
   > **or**

   Ever repeatedly hit (over at least a few minutes) or threatened with a gun or knife?
   > Yes No   If yes, enter 1 _____

8. Did you live with anyone who was a problem drinker or alcoholic or who used street drugs?
   > Yes No   If yes, enter 1 _____

9. Was a household member depressed or mentally ill or did a household member attempt suicide?

    Yes No   If yes, enter 1 _____

10. Did a household member go to prison?

    Yes No   If yes, enter 1 _____

Now add up your "Yes" answers: _____

This is your ACEs Score _____

Each "yes" answer scored one point. When the researchers correlated the results of the questionnaires with physical and emotional problems that their patients were having as adults, they discovered that ACEs significantly increased the likelihood of the following conditions/diseases during adulthood:

With Two or More Adverse Childhood Experiences:
- Autoimmune disease increased by 200%

With Four or More Adverse Childhood Experiences:
- Relative risk of chronic obstructive pulmonary disease increased by 260%
- Hepatitis increased by 200%
- Depression increased by 460%
- Suicidal ideation increased by 1,220%
- Teen pregnancy increased
- High-risk behavior increased
- Early paternity increased

With Six or More Adverse Childhood Experiences:
- Lung cancer increased by 300%
- Injection drug use increased by 4,600%
- Life expectancy was shortened by 20 years

With Seven or More Adverse Childhood Experiences:
- Ischemic heart disease increased by 360%
- Attempted suicide increased by 3,100%

The ACEs participants were 75% white, 11% Latino, 5% African American, and 7.5% Asian and Pacific Islander. Approximately 75% had attended college and their average age was fifty-seven. They were participants in the Kaiser Health Plan and were considered to be middle class. Only one-third of the participants had an ACEs Score of 0. One in six individuals had an ACEs Score of four or more, and one in nine had an ACEs Score of five or more. Women were 50% more likely than men to have experienced five or more categories of Adverse Childhood Experiences.

The ACEs—Follow-Up

The ACEs study has been extensively reviewed since its 1997 publication. Certain limitations to the study have been recognized. First, the average age of the participants was fifty-five to fifty-seven years. Thus, there may have been intervening issues for the participants between the time they were children and the time when they took the test; these were not measured. Second, there have been social and cultural changes in the intervening years that could generate different results.

In an effort to improve upon the ACEs Study, a subsequent study was conducted in 2013 to test and revise the list of Adverse Childhood Experiences from the ACEs Study.[xii] In the later study, 4,549 children from ages zero to seventeen years, living in the United States, were interviewed by telephone. The researchers concluded that, among other things, there is "… enough consensus that exposure to violence, sexual abuse and emotional mistreatment are harmful and likely have long-term health effects."[xiii]

In a recent study of 702 children, who were patients at the Center for Youth Wellness in San Francisco (the mean age of which was eight years old), Dr. Victor Carrion, a child psychiatrist and the director of the Early Life Stress and Pediatric Anxiety Program at Stanford University Medical Center, and Dr. Nadine Burke Harris, founder and CEO of the Center for Youth Wellness in San Francisco's Bayview Hunters Point, discovered that the patients with four or more ACEs were twice as likely to be overweight or obese and *32.6 times* as likely to have been diagnosed with learning and behavioral problems.[xiv]

In a 2017 study known as the "Parental History of Adversity and Child Well-being: Insights from Colorado," Professors Dr. Sarah Watamura and Dr. Samantha Brown of the University of Denver reported that the children of adults with at least one ACE were two to five times as likely to be diagnosed with attention-deficit/hyperactivity disorder or ADHD.[xv]

In other words, Drs. Watamura and Brown observed the intergenerational transmission of adversity.

ACEs and Divorce

But do all adverse experiences have to be ongoing or disastrous to qualify as ACEs? According to Andrew Garner, MD, PhD, FAAP, and a primary care pediatrician at University Hospitals Medical Practices in Cleveland, Ohio, "... people are beginning to realize that there is a spectrum of childhood adversity. Family circumstances that were considered routine—such as divorce or separation, parental mental illness or substance abuse, or growing up in poverty—are anything but. Whether the adversity is catastrophic or more routine and mundane, the effect on the body is similar. There's that common denominator of the physiologic stress response."[xvi]

Thus, when we apply the ACEs questions to conflict in our families or conflict as a result of divorce, they provide context that is relevant and important. In the heat an angry argument with the other parent or in the midst of your own pain, how likely is it that you or someone in your household will:

- Swear at your children, insult them, put them down or humiliate them?
- Threaten to physically hurt your children?
- Push, grab, slap or throw something at your children?
- Humiliate your children by arguing publicly at your children's school or sports events?

- Fail to tell your children that you love them and think they are important and special?

- Constantly argue with or criticize the other parent?

- Push, grab, slap or throw something at your spouse or significant other?

- Threaten your spouse or significant other with a gun?

- Drink alcohol to excess or use street drugs?

- Suffer from mental illness, depression or attempt suicide?

- Go to prison?

- Allow your children to have access to pornographic material or touch your children in a sexual way?

Some of the questions may seem remote to you, while others are quite relevant. It is not unusual for me to see clients who have a drinking problem or are using street drugs. It doesn't take much to lose control and hit a child. Mental illness and depression are quite common. Arguments between parents at children's sporting events or extracurricular activities are always humiliating for the children. And, when you are trying desperately to hold your life together, it would not be unusual to be preoccupied, and thereby make your children feel unloved or unprotected. Think about the parents who constantly criticize their children, abandon their children, or who alienate or turn their children against the other parent. In the story about Tim, we can identify at least five ACE's.

I can't help but wonder if the ACEs children are experiencing aren't reflected in current statistics. A recent report by the Centers for Disease Control and Prevention[xvii] noted that between 2007 and 2015, suicide rates doubled among girls and rose by more than 30% among teen boys and young men. There may be a number of contributing factors, but exposure to violence, including child abuse and neglect, bullying and peer violence, are associated with increased risk of depression, post-traumatic stress disorder, anxiety, suicide and suicide attempts.[xviii]

You may see this in your children. They may exhibit anxiety, ADHD, aggression, self-destructive behavior, depression, intellectual deficits and anti-social behavior. Should you be concerned?

Yes.

A lawyer friend of mine recently told me that she took the ACEs questionnaire on behalf of her deceased son. She was shocked to discover he had at least six ACEs. Her son witnessed his father's mental illness, depression and alcoholism. He witnessed his father's physical and emotional abuse of her and other women in his life. She left his father when he threatened to kill her. He watched on several occasions as his father was arrested and taken into custody. His parents were divorced.

My friend believes the ACEs her son endured charted a course for his life. He became an alcoholic. At age eighteen, he was killed in an automobile accident. He was the driver, and he was drunk.

My friend grieves every day.

Verbal Abuse—It Can Alter Your Children's Brains

Verbal abuse is an ACE, and research reflects how devastating it can be.

Is that possible?

What if you and the other parent just argue a lot? After all, you're not hitting your kids or molesting them.

What if you scream at them? Does that hurt your children? After all, you're not engaging in physical punishment—no spanking or slapping. You're not abusing alcohol or drugs, and you're not neglecting them.

Does merely exposing your children to verbal abuse between you and your partner hurt them?

Yes it does ... in damaging ways that you might never imagine.

Dr. Martin Teicher and his colleagues at McLean Hospital, Harvard Medical School, and Northeastern University conducted a study in which they concluded that high levels of verbal aggression can actually alter the trajectories of brain development in ways that increase the risk for substance abuse and other mental disorders in adulthood.[xix] In fact, Dr. Teicher observed that verbal abuse has the same impact as witnessing domestic violence or nondomestic sexual abuse. He concluded that it is a "potent form of childhood adversity."[xx]

The human brain is, of course, not fully developed at birth. Abilities and skills take decades to develop, and that development is guided by childhood experiences.[xxi] Verbal abuse from any source including parents, peers and siblings, leaves a structural imprint on a developing brain. Childhood experiences alter the physical structure of the brain and can result in an elevated risk of psychiatric problems.[xxii]

We have all heard the adage, "Sticks and stones may break my bones, but words will never hurt me." Perhaps this is where we get the idea it is acceptable to verbally berate others or fail to stop verbal abuse among children.

It's not okay.

I have worked with children who stated that the on-going, accumulative verbal abuse they received from a parent is the thing that, for their own survival, drove them away from that parent. In fact, they have stated that they might have preferred to be physically abused because their wounds would have been recognized and treated by the professionals, whereas the verbal abuse was not.

How tragic.

The verbal battering was ignored.

How preventable.

This is particularly sad because, in many instances, the parent who is the abuser is merely patterning the way in which that parent was raised and is unaware of the potential for the lifelong pain that he or she is inflicting on the child.

Well … we now have proof that words scar, and, once the words are spoken, they cannot be withdrawn. The damage is done. Verbal abuse is a form of childhood adversity and must be seen as one of the ACEs and treated in much the same way.

First, prevention: **STOP!** Then, seek out trauma-informed intervention, which is discussed in Chapter 4 and includes helping the child become resilient.

Abandonment—The Tear in the Parent-Child Fabric

Adrian listened to his parents argue.

It was a daily routine, and it scared him. But, he was only five and didn't understand why they didn't like each other.

Then one morning, his parents called him to the kitchen and made him sit with them at the table. They told him that they were getting a divorce. Adrian didn't know what a divorce was but continued to listen. Then his father said, "Who would you rather live with—your mother or me?" Adrian actually had no idea what he was talking about, but, because of his father's insistence, he weakly replied, "My mom."

At that point, Adrian's father stood up and walked out the back door. Adrian did not see him or hear from him for twenty years. Adrian spent his entire childhood in pain, and he could not stop thinking that he had done something wrong—something so bad that his father would leave. What had he done to make his father reject him? He waited for him at the front door, he hoped his dad would come to his school and he wished that he would call.

But, none of those things happened.

When they were reunited, twenty years later, Adrian's father apologized. While Adrian appreciated this, he could not get rid of the fear that other people he loved would reject him and would leave.

Adrian found his life partner at an early age and married her. He is now a creative webcast producer and attributes much of his success to his nurturing and supportive relationship with his wife. However, in spite of his personal and professional accomplishments, he still carries the scars of his father's abandon-ment with him and constantly fights his insecurity and inability to trust.

Abandonment has many faces, and, for a child to suffer from abandonment, a parent does not have to physically leave and never return. Some children stay with a parent who is constantly on the computer and ignoring them. Others suffer abandonment issues if they are not property clothed or fed or are ridiculed or held to unreasonably high standards or blamed for their parent's divorce. Obviously, if they are physically or sexually abused, they will feel abandoned and shamed. Abandonment can be an issue when one parent moves, without explanation, from the marital residence and without explaining how the children can contact them. Abandonment can also be an issue when one parent leaves just to take an unexplained break—particularly if the "break" is in close proximity to the parent's separation and is taken with a new significant other.

When children suffer from abandonment, they feel unworthy; they believe something is wrong with them, and that they are, in some way, inadequate. They become unable to trust others, to feel worthy or to experience intimacy. They may suffer from anxiety, depression or codependence. They lack self-esteem.[xxiii]

Child abandonment is considered child abuse in some states and must be reported by professionals who are consid-ered to be "mandatory reporters" and are required by law to report abandonment to the authorities. Penalties vary, but can range from fines, termination of parental rights, supervised access to the child and jail time. It can be serious for the parent.

Count it as an additional ACE. It can be devastating to the child.

Alienation—The Loss of the Parent/Child Relationship

One of the most devastating things a parent can do to children is to convince them that the other parent is bad, not trustworthy, and not deserving of their love and affection. Whether it's intentional or unintentional, subtle or overt, it is destructive because it robs the children of their right to freely love each parent and to feel loved by both parents.

In extreme cases, it robs the children of a parent.

However, alienation is often not clear cut. Some experts believe that alienation should be "viewed as a family relational problem rather than an individual [problem] of one parent or child."[xxiv] If the alienating behavior of the parents is reciprocal, that is when each parent is putting down the other, the children may distance themselves from both parents.[xxv] This is called the "boomerang rule."[xxvi]

Parents who strive for reunification often participate in reunification therapy together and, ultimately, with the child. But, the scars run deep. Some children are able to rejoin the rejected parent(s) when they become adults, but others are never able to reverse the damage. True alienation, alienation in which the rejected parent has been wrongly accused, is also counted as an ACE. When both parents are alienating, obviously, it is counted as an ACE.

Societal Conflict—It Should be Added to the List of Adverse Childhood Experiences

There are factors in society today that are unrelated to conflict in your home or to your divorce. They were not included in the original ACEs Study, but they add to the stress your children may already be experiencing.

Think about how children must face the ever-present violence in our society, including mass shootings and other vicious acts; the hundreds of murders that are played out on television shows; the rude, hostile, chaotic, and constant political news; the ongoing threat of nuclear war; the barrage of violent video games; aggressive acts at school; intolerance for minorities; sexually explicit ads; bullying and cyberbullying; and financial stress.

Our children live the in the "mass shooting shadow" and practice active shooter drills at school that are designed to teach them how to react if a shooter enters their building. In a recent TV interview, a student who survived the high school shooting at Stoneman Douglas High School in Florida, in which seventeen students were killed and seventeen were wounded, responded to a question.

The interviewer asked this student how she was dealing with the shootings. She stated that her approach to life has changed. Now, when she walks into a building, the first thing she does is look around and identify places where she could hide in the event of an attack.

If all of that isn't enough, we now have what Colorado's Governor John Hickenlooper has referred to as "state-supported child abuse." Regardless of which side of the immigration issue you are on, our children are exposed to pictures of small toddlers being pulled away from their mothers. They can tune into videos of children being held in wire cages. They hear reports that some children may never be reunited with their parents.

Surely this can be, for some children, a source of secondary traumatic stress that results from hearing about or observing the first-hand trauma that is being experienced by the immigrant children.

The American Academy of Pediatrics just announced new guidelines for pediatricians: to screen all children twelve years and older for depression. As many as one in every five teens experience depression at some time during their adolescence. The AAP recommends providing treatment teams, education tools, counseling, development of treatment plans and development of safety plans that would restrict lethal means, such as firearms, in the home.

This is the first time in ten years that the guidelines have been updated. It reflects the crisis that American teenagers are experiencing.

Is this really how we want our children to live?

Heartache—Although not Part of the Original ACEs Study—It's Real

Yes, heartache is real. It can be physically devastating, and we must acknowledge it.

When you tell your children about your divorce, be careful to observe their reactions. If they have friends whose parents are divorced, they may be familiar with the process and not appear to be overly concerned. Some children, however, will be shattered. They may clutch their hearts, or experience chest pain or vomiting. They may become depressed, lethargic or physically ill. One young teenager posted on his Facebook page, "My parents are getting a divorce. My heart is broken."

These symptoms may persist as your child grieves the loss of his or her intact family, a change in schools, the loss of friends or the loss of financial security. The sudden shock of your announcement, especially if your child has preexisting health problems, can cause your child to experience heartache, a very real physical condition that causes major changes in the heart and circulatory system.

Erv Hinds, MD, has studied and written about heartache and broken heart syndrome. "Children's symptoms," he writes, reflect a physical "change in the flow dynamics to the heart and other organs and an increase of [certain hormones] that will increase a child's heart rate, blood pressure, breathing rate, muscle strength and mental alertness."[xxvii] Additionally, the amount of blood that is pumped to the body each time the heart beats is significantly lowered, thus reducing the nutrients the body needs to function properly. It is this change in the heart that results in physical symptoms.

In his book, *Healing the Pain of Heartache*,[xxviii] Dr. Hinds notes that, while there are different types of heartache, acute heartache may result from a sudden tragic event, such as the loss of a loved one or a violent trauma. The loss of relation-ships and intimate connections or the loss of hope for the future can precipitate broken heart syndrome. Particularly significant for children is the loss of a parent, sibling, pet or divorce.[xxix]

Broken heart syndrome can be treated.

Be sure to inform your pediatrician of the crises your children are experiencing, so that your doctor can treat your children's emotional *and* physical health. Treatment will vary depending on the seriousness of the physical symptoms, of course, but may include monitoring blood pressure and psychological well-being, working with therapy animals, participating in a support group or prescribing medications. You must also inform the other professionals who have contact with your children, such as teachers, school counselors and coaches, who will need to know why your child's behavior may have changed.

Our society tends to believe, unfortunately, that children will "bounce back." We've often heard, "Don't worry about the kids, they'll be okay."

Well, we now appreciate that children are not automatically resilient. They can carry a lifetime of physical and emotional pain if they are not respected, loved and protected.

Resilience is a skill that you can teach your child.

Summary

The results of the ACEs studies have significant implications for all parents. This information must be shared, and it must be stated again and again: *unresolved parental conflict hurts your kids.* It creates immediate pain that can affect your children for their entire lives. When you add the increasing societal conflict to the mix, you have a perfect recipe for lifelong damage.

It's safe to say that many, if not most, parents do not understand the ways in which they can scar their children before, during and after a divorce. It is a time when people are passionate about being "right" and fail to consider any onlookers (i.e., the children, for example). It can be a very selfish time during which perceived parental survival trumps common sense. It's a time when it is easy to discount the stress that children experience from societal conflict and violence. For these reasons, it is incredibly important to plan ahead, design your parenting strategy and protect your children.

If your co-parent is unable or unwilling to work on these issues, however, it will fall to you to find ways to shelter your children and teach them resilience.

You will find suggestions in Section Two.

4

RESILIENCE—
The Good News

Helping Your Children Become Resilient

Resilience is the ability to recover from change, difficulties, misfortune and adversity.

Resilient children are those who can move from the pain of their parent's divorce and the unresolved parental conflict to a positive and successful position in their lives. By teaching your kids how to be resilient, you can actually change the outcome of their ACEs. Even if your children have only experienced positive stress or tolerable stress, learning how to be resilient can give them a remarkable life skill from which they can regulate their emotions and behavior; it will help them establish healthy relationships.

Some children are born with an ability to be resilient. Others must learn it. In either event, you can help your children develop resilience and guide them towards a successful adulthood.

Desmond Runyan, MD, DrPH,[xxx] an expert in the field of pediatrics and child abuse, notes that resilience includes the child's ability to learn and engage with his surroundings, the ability to regulate his emotions and behavior, and the ability to establish healthy attachment relationships—especially with parents and caregivers. According to Dr. Runyan, five protective factors can mitigate the destructive results of Adverse Childhood Experiences:

- First, your children will be better able to survive if they learn that stress is your problem, not their problem.

- Second, your children can develop resilience if they have mentors or other supportive adults who can reassure them, tell them they are fine and act as their defenders.

- Third, your children will do better if they can manage stress and function well, even when faced with adversity and trauma.

- Fourth, your children have an increased chance of overcoming ACEs if they have good temperaments. And

- Fifth, your children will be better able to survive if they are adaptive, clever and bright.

Some children have innate resilience. Others need to be taught. The challenge is to provide your children with the appropriate resources and to teach your children these skills.

In his national bestseller, *Hillbilly Elegy*, J.D. Vance beautifully summarizes the elements that allow children to become resilient.[xxxi] These include:

- Having a community that empowers children with a sense they can control their destiny

- Having access to a church [or other religious institution] that teaches lessons of love, family and purpose

- Finding emotional and spiritual support from neighbors

- Having family, mentors and lifelong friends who support and enable the children and show them what is available and what is possible

- Having a stable family member on whom the child can rely

- Having families that empower the children and give them a sense of control over their future

- Having someone who instills a lifelong love of education and learning

- Being surrounded by caring and kind men [and women]

- Having access to adults who can fix what is going on in the home

- Being able to define their dreams

John is a thirty-five-year old lawyer who is the epitome of a resilient human being. John grew up in a home with his mother and father until their divorce. He attended a Catholic school. However, he was brutally abused as a child. His father frequently struck both him and his mother. His father shouted obscenities daily and was often drunk. He pushed and shoved John. On one occasion, he pushed John into the engine hold of their boat and could have killed him. John's father was known to brandish guns and knives and threaten John and his mother.

John's parents ultimately got divorced. However, for John, the divorce was a good thing because his father left the home. He moved about thirty miles away and remarried. John's father insisted that John stay with him every other weekend. Amazingly, John tried to comply, but it was obviously very difficult for him. He suffered from anxiety and constant migraines, and the strain of the visits aggravated his problems.

When John was a teenager, he told his father that he did not want to travel for the parenting time, and he did not want to stay with him in an environment that was so unpleasant and stressful. They had not resolved the abuse issues and every other weekend parenting time was just too much for John.

John suggested that they see a counselor, which they did. Each of them went for two individual visits and one joint meeting. The counselor prepared John for the joint meeting, during which he confronted his dad. It was very threatening for his father to listen to John's grievances, and his dad ultimately stormed out of the meeting.

John and his father have not spoken in twenty years.

They exchanged two letters this year, but have had no other communication.

In a period of five years after his dad left, John's mother, grandmother, grandfather and best friend died.

Everything in John's past would suggest that he would fail in his life. He had too many ACEs, including physical abuse, emotional abuse, verbal abuse, the divorce of his parents and the death of four people in his life who were close to him.

But, no, his resilience was palpable. He put himself through college and law school and is now a well-respected attorney. He is one of the nicest people I know.

John survived his parent's divorce and the abuse. He believes that he has no residual psychological, emotional or mental health issues. He sees a counselor occasionally, does not have migraines, and has minimal anxiety issues.

Why was he able to survive?

His answer is consistent with the opinions of Dr. Runyan and J.D. Vance. First, he is adaptive, clever and smart. Second, unlike many children, he was able to maintain a positive disposition, in spite of the abuse he suffered at the hand of his father. Third, he had an amazing support system: his mother, his maternal grandfather, his maternal grandmother, his best friend and his school. Fourth, he had his faith, and, although he doesn't practice Catholicism today, he is a very spiritual person and takes time each day for morning and evening prayers.

Finally, he was able to get counseling.

Whether or not children can become resilient depends, in great part, on having families and friends to support them. It makes the role of the parents (and grandparents) enormously important.

In my book, *Parenting Plans for Families After Divorce,*[xxxii] I identify the ten best things you can do for your children to keep them away from toxic stress and develop resilience. To succeed, your children must have:

- Love and Support
  Children need to know that you love them uncondi-tionally and will be there for them—even if they make mistakes. Be present and be consistent. Empower them. You are the rock in their lives, and they need you to be there, so they can receive your love and give you their love. Having stable and consistent grandparents, extended family members, mentors and friends who can provide support is enormously helpful.

- Proper Parenting
  Your willingness to be a parent who will reach out for help from others to learn how to be a good parent, especially in stressful circumstances, is critical. Kids don't come with an instruction manual. Parents sometimes have to get help. It's okay—your children will benefit.

- Freedom
  Children need to be kids—to play, jump, dream, make mistakes and love. They cannot assume the role of the absent parent. They must be free to meet the challenges

of childhood and to gain a sense of control over their future. They need to be free to define their dreams.

- Time and Space to Grieve
  Children need to understand that it is acceptable to grieve and express their emotions. The loss of an intact family is huge. Additionally, your children may have to change schools, make new friends and adopt a new lifestyle, due to financial constraints. They must be able to grieve the loss of their former life; they must be able to express their emotions.

- Food and Necessities
  The financial needs of your children do not stop when you get divorced. Each parent has a duty to support the children. It can be overwhelming, but it is a priority. Children need stability and security. They need proper nutrition, sleep, medical check-ups and exercise. Their life will be different, and you will need to reassure them that the difficulties will be resolved.

- Education
  To raise strong, independent children, you must educate them and instill in them a love of learning. Make sure that they finish their homework. Get involved with their school. Talk to their teachers. Teach them to respect themselves and others, to take responsibility for their actions and decisions, to be honest, to cooperate, to keep commitments, and to love and sacrifice. You are their most important teacher.

- Rules and Boundaries
  Children need boundaries, and they need to understand the rules. Let your children know what is expected of them. Be consistent and predictable. It will make them feel more secure.

- Both Parents
  Children need both parents. You might have to structure the visitation to provide for their safety, but never make them choose between parents.

- Role Models
  Set an example. Bring other adults into their lives who will also act as role models. Show your children how to treat people with respect. They will model their behavior after you.

- Counseling
  If your child has experienced trauma, it is particularly important to seek out a counselor who is trained in trauma-informed care. The focus of this care is not, "What's wrong with you?" it is "What happened to you?"

Resilience can be learned and developed. We have all seen people who rise from adversity and persist when everything is against them. Think of people in your life who have overcome challenges to reach their goals and remain optimistic, even in the face of tragedy.

This is the gift you can give your children. They will be affected, in varying degrees, by the stress of your divorce. If they experience ACEs or any of the other events that cause toxic stress, it will be harder for them and they will especially need your support.

And they are not the only ones. As a parent, you probably need to work on your own resilience, in order to be a good parent to your kids.

Trauma-Informed Care/Counseling

Trauma-informed care is the type of counseling that is particularly appropriate when a child has experienced trauma. It is therapy that (1) addresses the trauma that a person has suffered, (2) understands the consequences, and (3) facilitates healing. According to the Substance Abuse and Mental Health Services Administration ("SAMHSA"), trauma-specific intervention programs generally recognize:

- The survivor's need to be respected, informed, connected and hopeful regarding their own recovery

- The interrelation between trauma and symptoms of trauma such as substance abuse, eating disorders, depression and anxiety

- The need to work in a collaborative way with survivors, family and friends of the survivors, and other human services agencies in a manner that will empower survivors and consumers[xxxiii]

Meet Lori Jackson, MA, LPC, RRT.[xxxiv]
Lori stands as a model for how to overcome trauma and maintain resilience.

In 1983, three-year-old Lori was kidnapped from her front yard. She was abused, dumped in a mountain outhouse and left to die. Three days later, a couple of birders who were in the vicinity heard her faint cry and rescued the near-frozen child. She survived the trauma, went to graduate school, married and, for many years, practiced as a therapist who used her own experience to help her clients. She is currently the executive director of the National Foundation to End Child Abuse and Neglect.

Lori's path wasn't easy, and she still works every day to make a conscious choice to let go and to fight off the sadness that comes from feeling like she is not doing enough to help others and to get through the pain that comes with trauma and ACEs.

She works every day to let go of other people's choices and make her own.

Lori received trauma-informed care, which means that she worked with professionals who could take into account the trauma she suffered and help her learn to cope with it. Trauma-informed care is appropriate when children have experienced damaging events. Interestingly, trauma-informed care begins with you, the parents.

According to Lori, the first and most important things you can do to help your children to overcome trauma and become resilient are to be **present** and **consistent** for them. Let me repeat: always present and always consistent, so they can count on you and never question your support. If your children have a secure attachment to you, any trauma they experience or experienced will be less destructive, and the long-term effects will be minimized. This is the first level of trauma-informed care, and it is critical if your children are to develop resiliency.

Next, you can help your children by allowing them to work with a qualified professional counselor. This may not be easy. First, you must support the idea of counseling; second, you must find a person who understands the impact of trauma on kids and can help them minimize the damage; and third, you must find a therapist that your children (and you) can trust.

In general, the therapist will focus on what has happened to the children rather than what is wrong with them. It is a different approach and one that is particularly important for children who do not have a secure attachment to a parent or other adult. The therapist must understand the ramifications of trauma and avoid judgmental attitudes that can cause additional harm to those who have survived trauma.[xxxv]

There are therapists who are specifically trained in providing trauma-informed care for adults and children. In Weld County, Colorado, the Department of Human Services, the Court, and North Range Behavioral Health obtained a $100,000 grant from Caring for Colorado. The goal of this program is to ensure that young children (prenatal to eight) and their families who are involved in the judicial and protective services systems have access to trauma-informed systems. You may want to contact your local Department of Human Services or mental health organization to explore whether there are similar services near you. Alternatively, you can contact the National Center for Trauma-Informed Care at 866-254-4819, *NCTIC@NASMHPD.org.*

Trauma-informed counseling can make all the difference for your children. Again, the question to ask is, "What happened to you?" rather than "What's wrong with you?"

Conclusion

Your children rely on you to give them love and stability. We know, without a doubt, that unresolved parental conflict can indelibly harm them. We know that, in many cases, this can be minimized or corrected. Even if you have experienced ACEs in your own life, and even if your children are experiencing ACEs and showing the consequences of toxic stress, you can change the outcome. Ultimately, it is not up to the lawyers or the judges or the other professionals. It is up to you, the parents.

But how? Read on. It's time to redefine your parental responsibility!

It's time to learn how to treat your children before, during and long after your divorce is final.

SECTION TWO

Taking Control Before, During and After Your Divorce

5

Preventing ACEs BEFORE Your Divorce

Successful post-divorce parenting is easier if you have plans in place and don't need to react in the heat of the moment. If and when a divorce appears to be inevitable, pre-planning will help you keep your anger away from your children. Here are some suggestions:

1. Create a Family Commitment Statement

The *Family Commitment Statement* is an important tool to define the way your family will work and grow before, after or even when there is no divorce.

Similar to a company business plan, the *Commitment Statement* recognizes that your family is important now, and will still exist, even after a divorce.

It answers questions like:

- What are your hopes and dreams for your family, including your Post-Divorce Family?

- What are your values, purposes and goals?

- How will you divide important the tasks among family members to achieve those goals?
- What obstacles must each family member overcome to meet those goals?
- How can you successfully work together, either as an intact family or a family of divorce?

To write a *Family Commitment Statement*, gather ideas from each family member (if you don't already have regular family meetings, this would be a good way to initiate the habit) then jointly write the statement. Periodically check to see if you are on track. It is a wonderful way to involve the children and to make sure their voices are heard.

2. Draft a Child Agreement

A *Child Agreement* **will reflect your shared or individual goals for the future and serve as a guide.**

A *Child Agreement* is a plan for how you will treat your children if you should ever get divorced.

You do not have to be divorced to make a Child Agreement. It's a plan you can make even if the thought of divorce has never crossed your mind. After all, you hopefully have a will—that's certainly good for future planning, even if you don't expect to die for some time. Unlike a Parenting Plan, which defines decision-making (custody), and parenting time (visitation), a Child Agreement may not be binding in court. However, it can be very effective in expressing your intent and serving as a guide in troubled times.

So, why not plan for troubled times?

What if you had an agreement that you and your co-parent designed in moments of peace, when divorce seemed a total improbability?

What if you firmly agreed, for example, that in moments of stress, you would not fight in front of the children? Wouldn't it be wonderful to have a way to protect your children? Interestingly, a prominent domestic relations judge, after hearing many divorce cases, believes parents should actually make this type of commitment at the time their children are born!

Before you even consider divorce, think about drafting a Child Agreement with your co-parent in which you make a commitment as to how you will behave should you dissolve your relationship. Generally, the breadth and specificity of any parental agreement, including the Child Agreement, will depend on the level of trust that exists between you and your co-parent. This may be difficult to gauge the farther out you are from a possible divorce, but all of these agreements are modifiable and should be revisited whenever circumstances change.

The provisions of a Child Agreement can be quite simple. For example, you might agree that:

- You will not engage in conflict in front of or within earshot of your children or, if you do, you will explain to your children how you resolved the problem.

- You will provide physical and emotional support for your children.

- You will listen to your children.

- You will not verbally abuse your children.

- You will always treat your co-parent with respect (even if you think it's not warranted).

- You will maintain and respect the privacy of your situation and will not share the intimate details of your divorce with the children or the community.

- You will keep your children out of danger.

- You will never abandon your children or let them believe you or your co-parent will leave them.

- You will not disparage, and will not allow others to disparage, your co-parent in the presence or within earshot of your children.

- You will not attempt to turn your children against your co-parent (even if you think that your co-parent doesn't deserve their love).

Your Child Agreement will serve as a beacon of reasonableness in the heat of a divorce. It can be as simple or as comprehensive as you like, but be certain it reflects your goals and values. It will make things easier for you and your co-parent and, most importantly, will benefit your children.

3. Enroll in Pre-Divorce Counseling

A good counselor can help you understand the emotional side of your divorce.

It can be extremely helpful to have a professionally-trained counselor or therapist listen to your circumstances and help you process how you and your co-parent can have a successful divorce and create a good co-parenting relationship. The counseling would not be for the purpose of reconciliation; rather, it would be to guide you through the emotional side of your anticipated separation or divorce.

For example:

- What are your goals?

- What can you expect emotionally from the divorce process?

- How should you and your co-parent tell the children?

- How can you work successfully with your co-parent?

Just as an attorney can handle the legal side of your divorce, a good counselor or therapist can help you with the emotional side. Pre-divorce counseling can be critical to a successful divorce.

4. Take Parenting Classes Before Your Divorce

Learn the skills you will need for good parenting before and after the divorce.

Many parents take parenting classes during their marriages. When you file for divorce, however, most states require you to take a Parenting After Divorce class before you can get your Decree of Dissolution. Unfortunately, by the time you take the Parenting After Divorce class, you may have already exposed your children to high conflict, fights and ongoing hostility.

By taking a class before you file for divorce, you will learn skills you need for good parenting both before, during and after the divorce. This idea recently became law in Singapore, where the parenting class must be completed prior to filing for divorce.[xxxvi] So, before you carry on in front of the children, learn how to take the conflict away from your kids. Learn how to communicate positively, productively and privately. You will absolutely save yourselves and your children from heartache and emotional scarring.

5. Design Your Post-Divorce Family

There is no "right" time to define your Post-Divorce family.

As with the Child Agreement, diligent and caring parents often collaborate, before a divorce, to define how their families will function in case of divorce.

Parties (and their attorneys) sometimes assume families dissolve when marriages end. However, families seldom completely disintegrate and, for the sake of the children, they should not. Even when parties live in separate homes and lead separate lives, both parents should continue to be part of their original family, at least as far as the children are concerned. The children's stability and security may depend on creating a fully-functioning, empathy-based and restructured Post-Divorce Family.

There is no "right" time to define the Post-Divorce Family. Some people recognize the importance of the family when they are drafting their Child Agreement or at the beginning of their divorce. Others reach resolution of family issues during their divorce and incorporate their ideas into their Parenting Plan. And some parties only begin to recognize the importance of the restructured family after the divorce is final and they have each moved on to a separate life.

The needs and circumstances of each family member will change over time, but if you are willing to support the concept of a restructured family, your children may find adjustment to be just that much easier. Your family is the only family that your children have known, and maintaining it will provide a framework for your children's security and safety.

6. Mediate Before you File for Divorce

Mediation is a process in which you hire a third party (the mediator) to facilitate the communication between you and your co-parent. The mediator, usually a lawyer or a mental health professional, will help you define the issues you need to decide and will help you create options for resolution.

Mediation is often required by the court after you file for divorce. However, it's quite likely that if you attend mediation for the child-related issues before you file, you can avoid disagreements. You might not want to use pre-filing mediation for financial issues if you have questions about your income, assets or debts. These issues can wait until after you file. However, identifying the best interests of the children before you file and coming to agreement on how you will make major decisions for them (custody) and how they will spend time with you (visitation or parenting time) is likely to save you time, money and emotional distress.

It will ultimately send a positive message to your children: that you are in control and that you love them.

7. Select Lawyers Wisely

Make sure your lawyer, if you have one, understands your goals and objectives for a peaceful divorce (which, for your children, should be what you want).

Today, many divorcing couples are choosing not to hire attorneys because they do not want to spend the money or they do not want to get into an adversarial situation that undermines their future co-parenting relationship. But going through the legal system without knowledgeable help can be both daunting and dangerous. You may create legal situations that will come back to haunt you simply because you did not know what you were doing or you did not understand your rights.

There is an answer.

Talk to several attorneys about your situation and plans. Many attorneys will not provide free consultations (don't be discouraged), but many do. You will benefit from a variety of opinions and approaches.

Talking to lawyers can be overwhelming; don't be intimidated. You are the one paying the bills; you have a right to have your needs met and to design your representation the way you are most comfortable.

So, think about writing your realistic goals and values down before you meet with an attorney. It will be an informative exercise for you, and it will allow the attorney to address your needs more coherently. When you interview attorneys, clearly state your goals and objectives for a peaceful divorce. Ask the lawyer about the lawyer's strategies for, and attitudes about, resolving conflict.

- Does the attorney appreciate and understand the importance of keeping conflict away from your children?

- Does the lawyer understand that you want to co-parent successfully after the divorce?

- Does the lawyer know about ACEs?

- Is the lawyer's conflict resolution style likely to   conform with or hinder your own style?

These are important questions. You will want to be represented by someone who knows the law, is willing to help you creatively settle your case, and is competent to represent you in court, if a court hearing is necessary.

8. Choose Your Divorce Team

Having a cooperative team of professionals (even if it's just a team of two lawyers) in your divorce can make all the difference.

A couple once came to me for mediation. The husband said, "We have put a great divorce team together." And indeed they had. They had each chosen an attorney, and they had made certain in their initial interviews that the attorneys could work together. They owned a successful business and jointly selected one person to value the business. They also jointly selected a therapist for the children and the mediator for the divorce issues.

We met several times in mediation, and the couple settled all of the issues. They were able to get a divorce that they both believed was fair to each of them. Their children were having difficulties, and it was important that the parents work together to help them. The parties did that very successfully and saved a considerable amount of money, compared to litigating the divorce.

Other possible team members might have included someone to evaluate the post-divorce circumstances that would be best for the children or financial counselors to address each party's post-divorce financial strategies.

You may not need a "team" to complete your divorce. But injecting "teamwork" will help you address issues that might otherwise cause problems later. The goal is to work with your co-parent and the professionals to complete your divorce in a way that is fair to each of you and is in the best interests of your children.

9. Think About Alternative Ways to Step Through the Divorce

There are many other types of professionals who can help you in your divorce.

Although it will always be the parents' responsibility to establish a positive tone for their divorce, there are many other types of professionals and service providers who can help you. To name a few, there are attorneys who specialize in collaborative divorce, a method in which parties agree their objective is to settle the case. There are mediators who serve as neutral third parties and will help you define the issues in your divorce and help you reach solutions. There are arbitrators who, if you agree to use an arbitrator, can act as a judge and make final and binding decisions in your case. There are attorneys who will work on a sliding scale. There are others who will help you with specific issues: this is called unbundled representation.

Bottom line: Explore your options and be creative. You and your children deserve to survive your divorce with the least amount of hassle and the greatest amount of caring.

10. Appreciate the Value of a Supportive Co-Parenting Relationship

The benefits go directly from you and your co-parent down to your children.

I recently had breakfast with a former client who wanted to discuss her new venture: becoming a divorce coach. During the course of the conversation, she related how she and her former husband had been able to maintain a positive relationship. Noting that it was not easy, they both had set their goals very high—for the benefit of their children. They wanted the best for their children and decided to be diligent and make choices that set examples for their kids. They treat each other with respect (even when it is difficult), and they value their children above all else. By their actions, they show their children how to hold their heads high and engage in positive problem-solving. My client stated that there are hidden benefits that "trickle down" to their children.

There is also the matter of mutual support. A few years ago, one of their children was critically injured. They had to make split-second decisions to save her life, and they subsequently had to work together to help her regain her health. They also had to be ever watchful and ready to help their older child, who witnessed the accident and suffered in his own way. My client said that they could never have been so successful if they had not been able to work together.

The path of divorce is not easy under any circumstances. However, everyone in your family will benefit if you and your co-parent can make a commitment to have a peaceful and supportive relationship. It is a worthy and worthwhile goal.

6

Preventing ACEs During and After Your Divorce

Protect Your Children from ACEs and Give Them the Gift of Resilience

Unfortunately (or sometimes fortunately), divorce happens.

It's the wise parent who can turn it into a positive experience for the children and parents. Once you decide to get divorced, you will have some decisions to make.

First, what do you want your divorce to look like? You and your co-parent can make an agreement to step through the divorce process with grace and dignity—for the benefit of your kids. It can be extremely difficult, but if you can maintain and strengthen your role as parents, you can enjoy the benefits of working together in your children's best interests. Your kids will be secure knowing that you are both in charge and that you will support each other (and them) when there is a problem. This can be painful, but it is critical if you want to protect your children from Adverse Childhood Experiences. It is critical if you want your children to be resilient.

If, on the other hand, you find your co-parent unwilling to cooperate in taking classes, making agreements or counseling, all is not lost, but you will be missing an important ally in protecting your children's well-being. Your challenge will be to assume a leadership role for your family. The following suggestions will be useful, even if you are going it alone.

Honor your children and yourself. Despite your pain, choose to adopt a constructive attitude and make choices that will protect them from toxic stress and give them the gift of resilience. There are many strategies you can use to create a positive environment for your children. Think about the following actions that you can take:

1. Reaffirm Your Commitment to Your Children

Use the occasion of your divorce to send a message of love and commitment to your children.

When your children were born, did you look at them and promise to always be there for them? Did you welcome them into your family and pledge to support them? Now you can do it again. Divorce gives you a break in the time and space of your life that you can use as an opportunity to restate your commitment to your kids.

This is a remarkably simple but amazingly significant point of passage in your life and in the lives of your children. Your recommitment sends a message to your children that says, "You are loved, and you are as special today as the day you were born." It is an important step for you, and it's staggeringly important for your children. If your co-parent can join you, so much the better—you'll both reaffirm your commitment to the kids. Show your children that you will be present and consistent for them—always.

2. Talk to Your Children About the Divorce

But shield them from intimate divorce details.

One of the most painful conversations you will ever have will be the conversation with your children when you tell them you are getting a divorce. For some children, it will be a relief. Others will be very aware that something has been wrong for a long time, and the announcement will not come as a surprise. Others will be broken-hearted. For all children, it represents the start of an enormous change in their lives.

Regardless of whether your children anticipate the announcement, there are ways you can handle the conversation to lessen the pain:

- If possible, speak to your children with your co-parent. They will need to hear the information from both of you.

- Generalize rather than blame. Share only the basic facts of the divorce with them, not the intimate details. Let your children know that divorce is a choice that neither of you anticipated or chose when you married. However, they should know that the divorce will be a reality regardless of either of your wishes. It is hard not to blame, but this is an adult issue … not a child issue.

- Tell them all of the things about your family that will remain the same after the divorce. Retain as much consistency as you can.

- If possible, let your children know your plans or, alternatively, let them know that you are still trying to decide on things and will keep them informed. At the very least, they should know if you or the other parent will be moving and how that will affect their lives. Give them timelines, if you have them.

- Let them know that it's okay for them to continue loving both of you and that both you will each continue to love them.

- Give your children informational updates as the divorce proceeds. However, keep divorce documents out of their reach. Those documents often contain information that is, and should be, confidential.

- Let your children know if you are planning to participate in mediation. Many courts require it, and many children have learned that that it is a way to problem-solve and avoid fighting.

- Let them know that you and your co-parent will continue to be in their lives—that they will continue to have you both as parents.

- Let them know that they are not responsible for the divorce.

- Keep talking. Your children's need for information and attention will not end just because the legal divorce is finished.

In your painful moments, you may be tempted to tell your children far more than they want or need to know about your situation. Be cautious. This is a time to protect your children and shield them. They really just want to know that you still love them and that you will continue to support and provide for them.

3. Keep Parental Conflict Away from Your Children (This is Not Negotiable)

Several years ago, I met with divorcing parents who were particularly unkind to each other. They couldn't control their anger, and they almost invariably involved their children in their fights. At the time I first saw them, however, the kids were doing relatively well.

Recently though, the same couple returned to my office to resolve some financial difficulties. I asked how the children were doing. "Well," the father lamented, "the older boy was flunking out of school, doing drugs and won't stay with his mother." The daughter was well on her way to having similar problems. It was obvious the parents had continued, despite our previous discussion, to involve the children in their adult problems.

During the most recent mediation, however, the parents agreed, at least, that they would get psychiatric help for their children. The irony was both maddening and overwhelming. The kids were identified as the patients who needed psychiatric counseling when, in reality, it was the parents who were creating the problems and needed the therapy. And so, two more children were lost in the circus of parental conflict. The parents successfully completed the legal aspects of their divorce, but they failed to protect the children in the process.

The lesson is clear.

When you and your co-parent need to discuss your relationship, particularly the divorce issues, take your conversation to another place, not just another room. In case you haven't noticed, kids hear through walls and are absolutely privy to hushed conversations. Agree with your co-parent that you will not discuss the divorce in any place where your kids can listen, and that you will not fight in their presence. Even if you can't agree to anything else, you must agree to this.

Period.

Unresolved parental conflict is too scary and divisive for your children to handle. To you, it's just an argument; to them, it can feel like life and death. They don't know where their loyalties should lie. Are they supposed to hate one parent and love the other? And, when you get over the pain (as you will), your children will still carry any scars you leave with them.

You can control where your disagreements take place, even if all you do is leave the building on your own. Ongoing, unresolved parental conflict is an ACE; it can create havoc for your children. Take the conflict away from them—take it out of their presence. And, by the way, if you are able to resolve your conflict and it is one of which the children are aware, let them know that, as adults and as their parents, you have worked out a solution.

4. Keep Societal Conflict Away From Your Kids (This Isn't Negotiable Either)

Parental disputes are not the only type of conflict that endangers our children.

Societal conflict does as well. It may be in the form of actual or threatened violence, such as bullying or cyber-bullying. More ubiquitous is virtual violence that enters our homes through television, the internet, video games and explicit recordings. Studies indicate that by the time a child reaches middle school, he or she may have witnessed as many as 8,000 murders and 100,000 other acts of virtual violence through various media.

Mobile internet access puts cyberbullying, virtual violence and pornography in the hands of every child with a smartphone or tablet. Virtual violence is in every movie theater and is easily accessed in shopping malls. Even seemingly benign media can be disturbing to children; this would include political ads, newscasts, prescription drug commercials that graphically explain possible side effects, and the ever-present threat of mass shootings, international terrorism and nuclear war.

The effect of these innumerable sources is cumulative and should be extremely concerning.

You will never be able to shield your kids from all threats, but even if your co-parent isn't cooperating, the two of you should be able to agree on the following obvious rules for your children:

- Limit the TV, movies and games they are allowed to play and make sure their choices are age-appropriate.

- Monitor and limit your children's use of smartphones and other mobile devices.

- Install parental controls on all TVs, computers and other devices that access the internet.

- Limit the time your kids spend on electronic devices.

- Talk to your kids about potential online dangers and what to do if they feel they are being bullied or contacted inappropriately.

- Don't allow pornography, violent video games or other explicit recordings, including music and spoken word, e.g., comedy, in your home, and protect your children from your own use of this media.

- Recognize that technology has become a much more dangerous place than when you were children, and that there are many dangers hidden in internet access and other seemingly harmless sources.

If your co-parent does not cooperate in protecting your children from these dangers, either pre- or post-divorce, it may raise legal issues you should discuss with an attorney or with social services. These dangers are real. There are limits on what the courts and other agencies can do; they have a lot on their plates. But you should not let yourself be bullied any more than you would allow your children to be bullied. Hopefully this will be a joint effort between you and your co-parent. It is critical that you work together to define the guidelines for your kids and that you cooperatively enforce them. It is another way to keep conflict and ACEs away from your children.

5. Communicate With Your Co-Parent

If your children know that you and the other parent talk to each other, they lose the power to manipulate you—they can go back to being kids.

Regardless of how you structure your custody (decision-making), your visitation (parenting time), your dispute resolution procedures, and your financial arrangements, you must learn to communicate with your co-parent.

Sounds sort of ridiculous, right?

After all, if you had been able to communicate with each other, you might not be getting divorced!

However, before your children are raised and gone, you will confront at least one situation in which they tell you an untrue story about the other parent or tell you only the half of the truth they believe you can hear or accept. You will need to confirm the information with your co-parent. When kids know that their parents actually talk to each other, they will lose their power and control.

It actually relieves them of a lot of responsibility ... so they can just be kids.

Additionally, you will have situations that will require your communication. You'll have scheduling problems or kid issues for which parental involvement is important. You'll need to share information about doctor's appointments, extracurricular activities and parent/teacher conferences—just for example.

Bottom line?

Communication becomes very important when you live in two homes, and it's easier if you develop a system.

So, now you have the challenge of creating a new system. Here's some suggestions:

- Limit your conversations to child-related issues. Talk only about what the kids need or want. Avoid discussions in front of the kids or where you might be overheard.

- Choose a communication means, be it text, email or telephone. Many people use an interactive computer program such as *Our Family Wizard* or *Talking Parents* to send messages and maintain a calendar.

- If you speak by phone, be thoughtful and considerate. Limit the conversation. If either of you becomes angry, end the call and call back within twenty-four hours. If you need to leave a message, be careful with your language and tone, and be certain you use a system the children can't access.

- If you text or email, again, be careful with your language and tone. Some people let their messages rest before pushing "send." Try not to be accusatory, sarcastic, defensive or provocative. Avoid pushing the other parent's hot buttons.

- Follow a precise format for all forms of communication. First, tell the other parent that you are calling or emailing about a specific topic. Succinctly explain the problem or issue. Offer your proposed solution, and ask for a response.

- If you receive a message, respond promptly either by (1) explaining your view of the problem or (2) telling the other parent that you have to think about the call/email and that you will reply within twenty-four hours. Then—keep your word. Return the call/email within twenty-four hours, and use your best efforts to find a solution to the problem. If activities occur during both parent's parenting time, don't consent to the wishes of your child before talking to the other parent.

- If communication problems persist, consider using a counselor or a mediator to explore the reasons for your miscommunications and set some guidelines. Failure to communicate with your co-parent can be extremely stressful for you and your children. It creates enormous amounts of anger—just the thing you're trying to avoid. So make every effort to make your communication with your co-parent as productive as possible.

6. Reject Domestic Violence—It is an ACE

Domestic violence is one of the most serious and potentially dangerous Adverse Childhood Experiences.

When children witness or hear a parent being abused, verbally or physically, they find themselves in an unimaginably vulnerable position. They and/or their parent might be hurt or killed. At the very least, they will be emotionally harmed.

If you are the parent in this situation, it is critically important that you protect your children and yourself by having an escape plan—before the violence happens. This might be running to a relative's house or to a safe house. If you believe that you are potentially unsafe, research the facilities that are available to you and be prepared to go to one if necessary. Have an emergency bag ready if you believe you will need to leave abruptly.

As remarkable as it may seem, sometimes victims of domestic violence are not aware of how dangerous their situation is. It isn't unusual for a victim to believe that he or she doesn't need help. They also might believe that their children, who witness their abuse, will get over it, which is unlikely.

So, if you are in a violent relationship, recognize the danger, and get help for you and your children.

In some counties, sheriff's deputies are trained to ask questions to screen for violence. These include questions like:

- Has the perpetrator ever used a weapon against you or threatened to kill you with a weapon?

- Has the perpetrator threatened to kill you or your children?
- Do you think the perpetrator might try to kill you?
- Does the perpetrator have a gun or can he/she get one easily?
- Has the perpetrator ever tried to choke you?
- Has the perpetrator ever tried to kill himself or herself?

If the victim answers "yes" to one or more of these questions, the officer makes a referral to the local crisis center. The officer calls the crisis center and asks the victim whether he or she wants to speak with a counselor.

Sometimes a victim refuses help because the victim believes that the situation will improve or get worse if they seek help. Sometimes a victim refuses help because he or she is financially dependent on the abuser or afraid that the abuser will turn on the children. All situations are tragic, and sometimes deadly. For children, they are devastating.

It's easy to recommend that victims get help. Sometimes they just can't. Those are the cases to watch—as neighbors and friends. Reach out. Call authorities. If possible, get help.

You may be saving lives.

7. Choose Your Children Over Alcohol and Drugs

Do it for yourself but, more importantly, do it for your kids.

Parental addiction is one of the most insidious problems that children face. It can easily destroy them. It is identified on the ACEs questionnaire—with good reason. Children cannot deal successfully with a parent who is drunk or high. They cannot count on that parent to show up and be present. It is embarrassing, and it is heartbreaking.

If you have an addiction problem, get help. There are many organizations, such as Alcoholics Anonymous, that can be of great assistance. It takes effort, and it takes perseverance. But if you care about helping your children become resilient, if you care about remaining a parent to your children, you must break the cycle and get sober. It's that simple. Choose your children over your addiction.

8. Understand Your Co-Parent's (and Your) Mental and Emotional Limits To Keep Your Children Safe

There are many forms of mental illness and personality disorders. If you and/or your co-parent suffer from an affliction, it is best to acknowledge it and plan your time with the children accordingly. It might be depression, anxiety, bipolar disorder, narcissism, borderline disorder or schizophrenia, just to name a few. Like alcoholism and drug dependency, living with a person who is mentally ill or depressed is on the ACEs list. It decidedly affects the children, and thus, it becomes important to keep them safe and help them understand the limits you or your co-parent might have. You may need the help of an attorney, a mental health specialist, or the court to determine how to deal with the situation. Your children might also benefit from counseling, so they can better understand the issues.

9. Adopt a Zero Tolerance for Bullying

Protect your children by monitoring their behavior and their use of electronic devices.

Be aware of your children's conduct outside of the home.

Are they being bullied?

Are they bullying?

Monitor your children's use of electronic devices and their potential for cyberbullying. Talk to your children. Be a resource for your kids. Be their rock. If they are experiencing bullying, you need to know about it, sooner rather than later. If they are bullying another child, you need to know about it. Work with the school, and help your school establish a no-tolerance policy when it comes to bullying. Have a no-tolerance policy in your home as well. Make sure that you and your co-parent are communicating and enforcing mutually agreed-upon rules in each of your homes. Make sure that neither you nor the other parent are bullying the children.

10. Agree on Rules for Disciplining Your Children

Hitting, Humiliating, and Threatening Your Children Are ACE's

When does discipline become an Adverse Childhood Experience? Parents step over the line when they humiliate their children or hit them or physically threaten them.

But, how can you design the way in which you will discipline your children? How do you coordinate your discipline with your co-parent to give resilience-building consistency to your children? How will you handle everyday discipline situations like failing to do chores, irritating siblings or otherwise being inconsiderate of others? How will you address larger concerns like acting out in school, engaging in inappropriate internet activity, failing to meet curfews or showing lack of respect for adults, including yourself or grandparents? Here's some tips:

- **Plan your strategy in advance and anticipate the inevitable problems.**
  If you can, identify with your co-parent or decide for yourself the limits of how far you and your co-parent are willing to go in allowing your children to experience the logical consequences of their inappropriate behavior. Family meetings, that you schedule to discuss your Family Commitment Statement, are a good time to involve your children in creating positive and well-understood consequences. The more potential problems you can anticipate, the better you will be prepared to handle them when they occur.

- **Identify appropriate punishments when things have cooled down—not in the heat of the moment.**
  It's best to include your co-parent, especially if your child spends time with him or her. That way, you can coordinate the discipline in both homes, and your child knows you are both on the same page and can't

be manipulated. Your children will get the message, and they will know that both of their parents are marching in the same direction for their benefit.

- **Get some guidance.**
  Remember the TV show, *Supernanny*? The visiting "supernanny" taught parents how to work with their children when they (both parents and children) were totally out of control. The supernanny demonstrated how to use effective discipline and how to set boundaries. If you have not seen it (and even if you have), it is worthwhile to find it on YouTube and watch a couple of episodes. It can provide great insight on how to discipline your kids without hitting them.

- **Don't allow anyone (including your co-parent) to hit your children, push them or otherwise humiliate them.**
  These are not an acceptable forms of discipline. They will scar your children, and they will scar the person who is inflicting the punishment. Once a parent resorts to physical discipline, he or she has lost control. Search for positive ways to modify your children's behavior and help them build resilience.

- **Let your children know that, right or wrong, you will always love them.**
  There will be moments when your children are being particularly obnoxious, when you are required, for example, to respond to their school or even bail one

of them out of jail. It is in those moments that you might want to run away as fast as you can or come down really hard on the child who is in trouble. Instead, institute EMR—Extra Mercy Required. When you recover from your anger or disappointment, your mercy may show itself in the form of goodwill, gentleness, kindness, forgiveness or generosity. Not too much mercy … just enough to let your children know that, right or wrong, you still love them.

11. Eliminate Parental Alienation

Alienation often requires two parents—don't be one of them

Alienation can occur when one parent (the "alienating parent") demeans the other parent in the presence of the children and attempts to turn the children against him or her (the "rejected parent"). The alienation can be nonverbal and very subtle, or it can be blatantly overt. It can be gradual but insidious. Perhaps a negative comment now or then about the other parent plants the idea in the children's brains that the other parent is bad. A disapproving glance is very effective for sending the message to the children that the other parent is not worthy of their love. Sometimes parents engage in outright threats such as, "You won't ever see your grandparents again if you stay with your mom/dad tonight."

On the other hand, the rejected parent can contribute to the problem by his or her behavior, basically confirming the accusations of the alienating parent. For example, the mother says the father is a jerk. Then the father steps in and acts like a jerk. Who is at fault? It's rarely clear cut, and because of that, situations can be very confusing.

Another situation exists when the parents each participate and denigrate each other. In those instances, the kids may distance themselves from both of you.

But this much is clear. Early negative childhood messages given by one parent to the children can become embedded in the children's brains, particularly if they are substantiated by the rejected parent's behavior. Sometimes parents or therapists can reverse the damage, but often they can't.

Robbing your children of the other parent, except in the most extreme circumstances, is cruel and unjustifiable. It can be as damaging and scarring as unresolved parental conflict. If you find yourself in the position of the alienating parent—stop. If you find yourself in the position of the rejected parent—stop. Run, don't walk, to a good therapist who can help you before the damage is irreversible. As much as you might disagree with and/or loathe the other parent, alienating behavior by either parent hurts your kids and cannot be tolerated.

12. Reject Abandonment—It is Not an Option

Let your children know you will not leave them

Kids, especially children who are in the middle of their parents' divorce, have a different perspective on abandonment. You may leave for a much needed weekend vacation or you may move out of the marital home to an apartment, and your children will be terror-stricken. All sorts of things may run through their minds: *Will Mom/Dad ever come back? Who will take care of us? Where did she/he go?*

It's just too scary.

It's best to prepare the children in advance if one parent is moving to a new residence, and it's best not to leave the kids—even temporarily—in the early days of the divorce. If you do have to leave, reassure them—let them clearly know that you're coming back. If possible, use online social media, such as Skype or Facetime, to let them know where you are and to keep in touch.

Your children may also experience a sense of abandonment when you consistently ignore them by working at the computer all day when they are with you.

They may feel abandoned when you bring a new "significant other" into their lives.

Sometimes parents think that the children will "just adjust." But it's not that simple. Your children may believe that you have chosen the new person over them and that you will leave them. If the new person has children, your kids, without their input or consent, will be expected to happily participate in the new "family."

The fact of the matter is, children are often not nearly as adaptive as we would like to believe. They will be hurt if their parent chooses another mate over their mother or father. They could be scarred if the new person doesn't like them or rejects them. They will make every effort to adjust (just to please you), but it's difficult to fit all the pieces together. Additionally, they will also experience another loss if you subsequently break up with this person.

Don't rush the introduction of a new significant other. Don't risk your children feeling abandoned—it's just not worth it.

Stay on track, and let them know that you are the parent, and you are not leaving. Not today, tomorrow or, if you can help it, ever.

13. Guard Against Parentification

Children should not assume the role of a parent or become a mediator between their parents

When parents fight, children often make enormous efforts to solve the problem. They may actually assume the role of the parent. They try to mediate and resolve all disagreements in the family, in an effort to keep the family together. They strive for peace.

It is destructive because, at a time when the children should be focusing on their own development and the resolution of their own emotional issues, they can end up taking care of their parents and siblings. It is remarkably enervating for them and is yet another important reason why parents must remove the children from parental conflict and place the children above all else.

14. Allow Yourself to Grieve

It is important to acknowledge where you are in the grief cycle and where your co-parent is as well.

When you experience a loss, it is likely that you will transition through the grief cycle and experience denial, anger, bargaining, depression and acceptance.

In a divorce, you must potentially deal with the loss of your marriage, the loss of an intact family, the possible loss of a relationship with your co-parent's family, the loss of a financial plan for the family, the loss of friends, and the loss of your dream of living happily ever after. Any one of these things will take you involuntarily through the grief cycle.

However, a problem that couples experience is the fact that they individually find themselves in different and opposite stages of the grief cycle, which creates issues. For example, when you are angry, your co-parent may be depressed; when you are accepting the situation, he/she may be denying it.

Is it complicated? Very.

For your children's sake, acknowledge where you are in the grief cycle and where your co-parent is as well. Try to recognize that your co-parent's denial, anger, or depression may have nothing to do with you but, rather, have everything to do with where he/she is in the grief cycle, and you may be the last person who is able to affect it.

To protect your children, help yourself and enhance your relationship with your co-parent:

- Recognize and acknowledge your stage of grief.

- Recognize and acknowledge your co-parent's place on the grief scale.

- Recognize you can't control your co-parent,

but you can give your co-parent space to move to the next level.

- Recognize the need for professional help. If you or your co-parent gets "stuck" in one stage, think about getting help from a counselor. It's easy to ignore these signs, but your children will know and will be affected.

- Love and embrace your children. Protect them. Separate them from your adult emotions and those of your co-parent.

- Create a safe and sane environment for your children. Recognize that you are the only person you can control.

15. Allow Your Children to Grieve

Your children will also experience loss and must be allowed to grieve.

Just as you go through the grief process, your children will also experience significant losses on multiple levels, including the loss of family, unified parents, financial stability, school, home and friends, trust, and the loss of safety that you as parents may have provided.

Your children may not know how to express their fear, distress and other emotions constructively. Sometimes they will be rude or act out in school. They may engage in antisocial and unpredictable behavior. They may not be able to handle conflict. Older children may act out sexually. Delinquency and drugs and alcohol use may rise, and there may even be an increase in suicidal ideation. They cry out for help, and you, the parent, must respond.

Work with your co-parent to let your children know you are both there for them. Counseling for your kids will give them a place where they can speak unguarded. Work with the school, and alert their teachers, counselors and coaches. Allow your children to express their hurt to you and your co-parent in a constructive way. Assure your children again and again that "this too will pass."

Committing to your children, loving them, embracing them, and protecting them will build resilience.

16. Build a Network for You and Your Children

Your network can be your lifeline

One of the striking and consistent things we see in JD Vance's book, *Hillbilly Elegy*, and in the work of Dr. Des Runyan, as discussed in Chapter 4, is the importance of having family, mentors and lifelong friends to support and enable children.

Adults need a community of supportive friends as well.

Resilience is built by being appreciated by others. Encourage your children to recognize and do things for people and organizations in your community. No opportunity or task is too small to generate appreciation, especially for those in closest proximity. Simple gestures such as shoveling a neighbor's walk, raking leaves or baking cookies will make your children feel that they are contributing. Being appreciated by others builds confidence and self-esteem. It is a way to continue your effort to build resilience.

There will be times when you need to reach out for help. You may need special assistance from one of your children's teachers or a ride for your children from another parent. Little favors are easy to ask for and receive if you have built your network and have done nice things for others. It's always pleasant to give, and others will be happy to return favors, which, in turn, makes it easy to receive.

Your network may become your lifeline, so keep reaching out; keep doing things for others. You and your children will feel safer knowing there are others who are watching out for you and can help all of you when you need it.

17. Maintain Privacy—for the Sake of Your Children

Broadcasting your situation to others will ultimately hurt your children

David and Marsha were a newly separated couple when I met them in mediation. Marsha had emotionally left the marriage long before, and she had become involved with another man. David was crushed and could not contain his grief and pain. He ultimately went to the children's private school and shared the intimate details of Marsha's affair with the children's teachers and parents of the children's friends. The children, of course, heard about it and were humiliated. It became an impossible situation for them, and they ultimately felt compelled to change schools.

There is nothing as comforting as having the support of your friends and relatives during your time of crisis.

But be cautious.

As hard as it is not to share intimate details, your children must face the same community, and it will be humiliating for them to know their friend's parents or their relatives know the details of their parents' divorce. Don't indiscriminately broadcast your situation to just anyone who will listen. You will regret it later, and you will hurt your children. Again, if you are sharing information about your divorce, even with someone you trust, take the discussions away from your children. Don't let them overhear your conversations. If your children tell their friends and parents who, in turn, ask you about the situation, you can just respond that you are handling it with your co-parent (but thanks for asking).

18. Be a Steady and Consistent Parent

Be a person your children can trust

If you want to teach your children how to be resilient, then show them—be predictable.

Always be there. Be present. If you say you're going to show up—show up. Never give your children reason to question your loyalty or devotion to them—even when they are acting out or appear not to care. The experts agree: being a steady and consistent parent is one of the most important ways you can help your children develop resilience.

19. Be an Advocate

Protect your children

Your children need to know you will always be on their side and that you will always love them (even when they are obnoxious and test your patience).

They need to know that you are their advocate and that you will protect them. This may be at home, in school, at the doctor's office, in the neighborhood, in the community, even in the legislature. So, be a Mama/Papa Bear and get your game face on.

March for your children!

20. Be the Bridge

Be a mediator for your children

There will be times when you will need to be a bridge or mediator between your children, their friends and other adults (including your co-parent). Be prepared to handle all situations that arise, and to contribute to solutions for all shapes and sizes of problems. Your children cannot do it alone.

They need a role model.

They need a bridge.

You will also be teaching your children how to mediate disputes for themselves. Problem-solving is a major component of resilience. Learning these skills will help your children confront the challenge of your divorce as well as other issues that they will face in the future. They will learn to be the bridge.

21. Listen to Your Children

Be observant. Watch your children and hear their cries for help

Children speak to us in many ways. During your divorce, you may notice your kids are having trouble in school or, just the opposite, they get super diligent. They may start bullying others, argue incessantly with their siblings or have repeated temper tantrums. They may cry a lot or become depressed. They may cling to you or they may push you away. Anxiety attacks are not uncommon. Some children are able to express their fears, their anger, or their sadness. Others cannot and turn to drugs, shoplifting, vandalism or worse.

Your children will find different ways to speak to you, either through their behavior or their spoken messages.

As a parent, you must be constantly vigilant. You must place your children's best interests ahead of your pain and guide them. Provide resources for them. These may be relatives, clergy or counselors. They will reach out in some way. Their voices are important.

Listen to your children.

22. Praise Your Children

Praise Supports Resilience

When your kids do something good, helpful or considerate, let them know that you've noticed it and that you appreciate them and their behavior—even if it's just the tiniest of things. Praise leads to positive acts that lead to more praise. It will keep your kids moving in good directions, and with praise comes resilience.

23. Create Boundaries

Children feel safer when they know the limits

Whether it's crossing the street as a four-year-old or avoiding dangerous sites on the internet as a thirteen-year-old, children want to know the limits. You can make this part of your Family Commitment Statement, or you can just set boundaries as the need arises, but let your kids know the limits. Let them know the line. And let them know the consequences if they cross the line. Knowing how far they can push you is part of the consistency in their environments that will add to their resilience.

24. Love Your Kids

Love doesn't cost any money so give it freely— be generous

Love, love, love. Can't give enough … can't get enough. Open your heart.

7

Prevent ACEs by Taking Control of Your Co-Parenting

It is sometimes evident to me, during the course of mediation, that many parents try to skirt their co-parenting responsibilities by dividing custody (decision-making). They might, for example, decide that one parent should make all the medical decisions and one parent should make all the education decisions. Or, they give total decision-making responsibility to one parent. I believe that the idea behind these approaches to parenting is that the parents will have less contact, and thus less conflict. It rarely works that way.

Whether you call it sole custody or decision-making, split custody, shared custody or allocated custody, parents still have to work together and talk to each other. And it's the parent's responsibility to arrange how that will happen.

There are things that you can do that will make co-parenting easier. Please consider the following:

1. Talk to Your Co-Parent

It's not a choice

If you want to give a gift to your children, learn to speak (communicate) with your co-parent. Sometimes it is really difficult, if not impossible—but it's not a choice. You need to rise to the challenge of parenthood, and, in order for your kids to be secure and to be free to succeed, you need to take this level of concern off of their shoulders. In order for your children to be free, they need to be able to count on their parents to behave with respect for each other. They need to be able to count on their parents to take responsibility for parenting.

2. Check Out Your Kid's Stories

Children become adept at splitting the truth or lying so they can please both parents

Children will do anything they can to please you and to avoid conflict.

I once had a client who wanted to take his daughter on a trip. She told him that she couldn't go because, if her mom knew that he was bringing his girlfriend, she would be furious. She told her mom that she didn't want to go because her dad was bringing his girlfriend, and she didn't like her. The truth was, the daughter just didn't want to go to the location that the father had chosen.

Both parents were angry, and it wasn't until they sat down in mediation and exchanged stories that they figured out that their daughter was telling each of them the part of the truth that they could believe or accept. It's called "truth splitting," and kids do it all the time.

Children will sometimes go beyond truth splitting and simply lie.

Many parents have told me, "My child would never lie." Unfortunately, though, kids will often resort to lying as a protective measure. Sometimes they feel that they need to lie so they won't get in trouble or so the other parent won't get in trouble. They usually know they are lying and do it out of desperation. It works, however, only if the parents aren't communicating. By communicating with your co-parent, you can lessen your children's desperate need and ability to lie.

It will be a great relief to both you and especially your child.

3. Arrange Nontoxic Parenting Time Exchanges

This is another way to keep conflict away from your children

If you really can't tolerate being around your co-parent, arrange Parenting Time (visitation) exchanges that don't require direct contact in front of the kids. A strategy that judges use is to schedule the exchanges/pick-ups after school or day-care. It's a good way to keep conflict away from the kids. If school is not in session, jointly pick another neutral site where there is supervision and where the kids can be dropped off by one parent and picked up by the other. This might be at the home of a friend, relative or short-term babysitter. Many organizations have professionals who offer this option along with other post-divorce services. If you do have to see your co-parent at the exchanges, don't discuss any divorce issues and, of course, avoid conflict.

4. Send Messages to Your Co-Parent—but Not Through the Kids

Children are terrible messengers—don't even ask them

Children are not good at delivering messages.

They often don't understand the message or they get it confused when they try to restate it. They are not comfortable being placed in the role of translating parental messages. And they often fail to deliver them, which causes unending conflict between their parents.

What's the solution?

Never ask the kids to carry messages, no matter the child's age or how trivial the matter. This includes asking your children to deliver the child support check to your co-parent. It places your child in an extremely awkward position, and it increases the possibility for conflict between you and your co-parent. It is a major stressor for your children.

However you decide to communicate, make sure that you and your co-parent do not involve your children. The child support check can be mailed. The soccer schedule can be emailed. The doctor's report can be texted. Do anything to communicate, but don't do it through your children.

5. Go to the Parent-Teacher Conferences

Spare the teachers—don't ask for separate conferences.

Have one conference with both you and your co-parent present. You will both hear the same information, given at the same time, so there is less chance for misunderstanding. Information won't have to be repeated and potentially misstated. Your kids will save face with the teacher, i.e. the message from your child to the teacher is, "My parents are divorced, but they work together!"

It's important for the well-being of your children, and, by the way, they will appreciate your willingness to be a part of their school life. It reflects your love and caring. If one parent can't attend the conference, the other co-parent needs to provide the information to the absent co-parent in a timely and objective manner.

6. Remember and Share Special Events

Help your children celebrate both parent's special days

It's hard for children to remember each parent's birthdays, Mother's Day and Father's Day. Help them remember. Help them make a gift for the other parent. They can easily create a little book or a card with a special message. It makes the children know that they are free to support and love both parents. And—it reinforces the co-parenting relationship that you want to have with the other parent.

7. Share Travel Plans

If possible, let your co-parent know if you intend to travel with the children out of your home state, with the understanding that your co-parent will not bother you except in case of an emergency. The fact is that a parent starts to panic if he/she doesn't know where the children are. Before you leave, give the other parent your itinerary (including airline schedules), and where the children can be reached, only if there is an emergency.

The kids will feel safer if they know that both you and the other parent are watching out for them.

8. Stay in Touch With the Children

As a general rule, a parent likes to speak, Skype or Facetime with his/her kids when they are at the other parent's home.

It's okay as long as you don't disrespect the other parent's time with your children. So, limit the times that you speak and the duration of your call. You might make arrangements to text your kids. Your children should be able to contact either you or the other parent at any time (within reason). Communicating with your children while they're at the other parent's home can be a point of important connection. But, because it can also be another source of parental conflict, it's best to define the rules and stick with them.

9. Attend Doctor Appointments

You will get their medical information firsthand

In many situations, one parent makes the doctor and dentist appointments for the children. If you both want to make them, you will need to coordinate that. In any event, unless your situation is unusual, you will want to keep the other parent informed of the time and place of appointments.

Often both parents attend, but professionals really don't want to hear any parental conflict in their offices.

10. Carry Identification Cards

It's a good idea to keep a note in your wallet or billfold that directs the finder to call the other parent if there is an emergency situation, such as a car accident or national crisis, in which you and the children are involved. It, of course, contains the other parent's phone number and perhaps email address. My clients started doing this after 911, and they have continued doing it because it makes sense. If the parent with whom the children are staying is hurt, the other parent needs to get the children.

11. Maintain Contact Forms

It's important to keep any parental conflict out of the children's school or camp setting.

Unless there are reasons to limit contact, both parents should be named on the school and extracurricular records and both should be contacted if there is a problem or event. The schools, camps and coaches should send announcements to both parents. Some camps will not allow a parent to pick up the children unless they are listed on the contact form. So, get the records straight and keep them up-to-date.

12. Help with Homework

It seems obvious, but I have seen many parents fight over their children's homework.

Was it completed at the other parent's home?

Was it done correctly?

Was it actually turned in to the teacher?

Your children need your support—in both homes. They need to know that you and the other parent will both hold them accountable for the work they do in school.

So, be sure that all assignments are completed at your house and that they are completed at the other parent's house. Most school districts have a parent portal on which you can check assignments and grades on a daily basis. If there is a problem, work with the other parent to figure out the source of the problem:

Are your children giving you the right homework assignment information?

Are they completing the assignments?

Are they actually turning in the homework to the teacher?

Does a child need a tutor—have you discussed this with your co-parent?

If necessary, contact the teacher and attend a joint meeting with the teacher. Success in school is critical to your child's success in life, and it's important that you identify problems right away to avoid potential future failures.

13. Discuss Religion

Religion is easiest if both parents agree on the children's participation.

Many fights have been sustained in the name of God, and your children don't need to be part of further conflict. If you agree that they may attend the services of a particular religion, let them attend in peace. You will also want to discuss how much religious training is appropriate, if any. If the children have a religious event, such as a communion or Bat/Bar Mitzvah, discuss the logistics and financial arrangements with your co-parent.

Try to agree—disagreement leads to mountains of pain for the parents and for the children.

14. Go to Extracurricular Activities—but Don't Embarrass Your Children

Some parents have such a hostile relationship that they can't attend their children' extracurricular activities without incident if the other parent is present. It's hard to listen to the stories I hear about extracurricular activities:

Will Dad bring his girlfriend?

Will Mom bring her lover?

Will the parents have a fight in front of the coach and the other parents?

Will one parent not be allowed to attend?

Will grandparents or other relatives attend, and what are the expectations?

Who will take the child home from the activity?

It's amazing the number of variations that parents have devised.

But here is the bottom line!

Your kids want you to be proud of them, and they want to show off a little for their parents. Don't rob them of that opportunity. Success is wonderful for their egos and supportive of their enormous efforts to become a fabulous human being. Having their parents present to witness their successes (and failures) is like frosting on the cake. But you must absolutely behave so that your presence is not a distraction or an embarrassment. Humiliating your children is an ACE, and it's critically important to avoid this situation.

15. Choose Counselors for your Children, If they Need Help

Children often benefit from having a person in whom they can confide. It gives them a moment of peace in their otherwise confusing lives. However, you must find a really competent counselor with whom the child can connect. After all, this person will be treating your child.

You can find a counselor by asking around—ask your friends, co-workers, lawyers. Compare notes, and see if you're getting the same person or persons on both your lists. Then interview the therapists. Check references, if possible. Ask what the treatment plan might be. Ask if you will be involved in the counseling. If your child has suffered an ACE, seek the help of a trauma-informed counselor. At the end of the day, you will need to have confidence in the person you choose, so do everything you can to make a good choice. If I doesn't turn out as you had hoped, you can change counselors, but this is sometimes hard on your kids. It is best to check everything out before your child starts sessions.

16. Stay Ahead of the Game

Get real—step up to the plate—support your kids

Having children, as we well know, is expensive. There's no way around it. As a parent, you must stay ahead of the money game. If you don't already have a job, get one—even if it is in a position you consider beneath you. Work hard, get paid and participate in supporting your kids. It's hard to be resilient if you are worrying about your next meal or how your parents will pay the rent or mortgage or whether or not you will have lunch money.

So, step up, reach out and help.

17. Participate With Your Child

When your kids are with you, be with them.

Out of your total life span, approximately seventy-nine years if you're lucky, you will spend only eighteen of those years being with your children most of the time.

That said, there will be days that feel as though they have forty-eight hours. But, truly, you will blink, and your children will be off to college, the military, getting married or getting a job to be on their own. Your goal is to raise children who can move on to the next stage of their lives and be happy and productive.

It's safe to say that parenting, under the best of circumstances, doesn't come with any guarantee for success. But, if you want to give your children the greatest chance for success, be "present" with them during those eighteen years. Go to school and extracurricular events. Attend parent/teacher conferences and doctor appointments. Play with your children—throw a ball, workout, fish, ski, run. Plan events and coordinate them with the other parent. Pay attention. Put your iPhone and your computer away. Talk. Enjoy. Be with your kids.

You only have one chance.

18. The New Significant Other—Be Thoughtful

The introduction of a new significant other will change the balance of your parenting relationship—sometimes for better and sometimes for worse

You meet someone new (or perhaps you met him/her before the divorce). It is inevitable, but there are lots of ways that you can enjoy time with each other without involving your children. Kids in divorce spend a lot of energy adjusting to their new life and grieving the loss of their old life. They don't need to know early on that one of their parents has found a new "mother" or "father" for them.

While there is no defined length of time you should wait to introduce the new person in your life, observe your kids and gauge whether they are ready. How are they doing? It may be months or it may be sooner. Most importantly, when you do think that it's the appropriate time to introduce your children, let the other parent know (in advance) that you will be arranging a time for this meeting, so he or she has some prep time and can respond appropriately to the children when they bring home the news. Discuss with your co-parent whether he or she wants to meet the "significant other" and how this should occur.

Each situation is different and there are no cookie-cutter answers as to what is right and what is wrong.

19. Use the Professionals

Many professionals offer very creative services that can be extremely valuable in helping you deal with your divorce. They may have different titles in your state, but look for ones that provide the services you need. Here are a few of them:

- **Counselors**
  Counselors (therapists) can help you learn to work with your co-parent, even if your co-parent does not want to participate or help you deal with individual issues. You may want to take the children to separate counselors to help them cope with the changes in their lives.

- **Parenting Coaches**
  When parents separate, they often assume roles that are unfamiliar to them. If either parent needs assistance developing parenting skills, a parenting coach can be extremely helpful. Sometimes parents meet separately with the coach, and sometimes the coach comes to the house to observe the parenting style of either (or both parents) and give them guidance. The coach's responsibilities may vary, depending on your particular needs but can include parent education, parent-child communication, training and co-parent conflict resolution training.

Be sure to carefully define what you need from the coach.

- **Parenting Coordinators**
  Making decisions with your co-parent about your children, even minor ones, can be difficult. The parenting coordinator, as the name suggests, can assist you in resolving conflict and implementing your parenting plan.

- **Parental Responsibility Evaluators**
  The Parental Responsibility Evaluator (PRE) conducts investigations and makes recommendations to the Court regarding parental disputes and child issues. The PRE will often interview the children and adults who have significant contact with the children. The evaluation may include psychological testing and can be expensive.

- **Child and Family Investigators**
  To avoid the high costs of a full-blown PRE, some states allow for the appointment of an expert with more limited authority. The Child and Family Investigator (CFI) (sometimes called a Guardian ad Litem (GAL) investigates and reports to the court on any issue concerning the best interests of the children. This position may not be available in all states.

- **Substance Abuse Evaluations**
  Alcohol and drug assessments may be made as part of

another evaluation or a stand-alone service by a psychologist or other professional.

- **Mediators**
  A mediator is a neutral third party who is hired to meet with you and the other parent to help you identify the issues you must decide in order to get divorced and to help you both reach resolution on those issues. Mediators may be lawyers or non-lawyers. The process is confidential and nonbinding, unless you agree otherwise.

- **Arbitrators**
  Arbitrators resolve disputes and issue opinions, much like judges. The decisions of the arbitrators are generally final and appeals are limited to certain statutory issues. The process is private.

It's very difficult to resolve all the issues of your divorce without some help. However, it's a good idea to decide the kind of help that you need and the amount of money you will pay. Create a budget and work within that budget to put your team together. You may need very little help, or you may need a lot. Remember, anger is expensive, but if you need help … you need help. You may need to ask the Court to order the services of a professional.

20. Avoid Conflict Over the Little Things

Be careful—the little things matter

You're creating a new life and changing the relationship that you once had with your co-parent. There are, however, things that you can do that will make the other parent go berserk. For the sake of the children (remember you're trying to keep conflict away from them), here are some tips:

- Always be on time for the Parenting Time/Visitation exchanges. Have your children ready. If you are delayed, call the other parent and give an estimated time of arrival or time you will have your children ready.

- Send clean (and appropriate) clothes with your children when they go back and forth. Always return the clothes (in clean condition) that the other parent sends.

- Tell the other parent if you want your children to bring clothes for a special event and let your children and the other parent know the nature of the special event. It's fun to anticipate.

- Let the other parent know in advance if your children will be spending time with your significant other. It's not fair to let your children break the news to the other parent.

- Don't make disparaging remarks about the other parent (and this goes double for your family members and your significant other). Do not allow your children to become participants in your problem.

- Let your children spend real time with you. They do not have to be entertained all the time. Give them chores. Read to them. Help them with their homework. By sharing the hard work, they will relate to you as a parent—not as a deep pocket.

- Tell the other parent about remarks your children make that cause you concern. It can help clarify problems, and it will send a message to your children that their parents (both of them) are still in charge.

- Coordinate things, such as bedtime and special diets, in both homes.

- Go the extra mile. Be a good role model—even if no one thanks you for it. Your reward will be in knowing that you have given your best to your children.

8

Taking Control of Your Life—Just You

Make Your Life Easier

So now you come to the fun part. This chapter is for you—
and only you. No co-parent to acknowledge. No kids to watch.
No legal stuff. You will find ideas that can make your life
easier and hopefully happier. Enjoy.

1. Claim Your Value—Give Yourself a Hug

You deserve a hug today

Parents often go unappreciated. After all, you're *expected*
to be good. Yup, you make the meals, clean the house, schlep
the kids, go to work, and look great while you're doing it!
Families are notorious for taking parents for granted. You can
always ask for recognition, but that takes the fun out of it. So,
perhaps, you need to toot your own horn and claim your
own value. Make an announcement. In fact, make several
announcements, and then repeat them. Let your kids know
all the good things you do for them and for others. Let them
know that you would like a few attaboys. In any event, recognize

yourself for the wonderful person you are and the thoughtful things you do. Give yourself a hug—really!

2. Control Your Attitude

Determine what you want and determine how you will get it

Wise people have said that the only thing you control is the attitude with which you approach a situation. Well, it's true and worth repeating. You determine what you want, and you determine how you will survive. Please read Victor E. Frankl's *Man's Search for Meaning*. If you haven't read it, it describes how to overcome severe challenges in life. The book has the power to change your life. It changed mine.

3. Grab a Branch and Hang on Tightly

If you fall into a river and are being swept away, you instinctively grab for a branch or for anything that will keep you from drifting into oblivion. You must do the same in your life. If you have "fallen," you must reach out and find someone whom you can hold tightly. It might be a friend, a religious leader, a relative or perhaps a therapist. Don't hesitate.

Most people are more than happy to help you—especially if they can see you are really trying hard to solve your problems.

4. Be Present for Your Children

Do not abandon your children—keep doing everything you can to participate in their lives

It's hard to live in two homes.

It's painful not to be with your children. Your kids' lives go on, and sometimes you will feel like you're not a part of those lives. It's expensive to support two homes, and things you might have done with your kids during the marriage can get tossed aside because you can't afford them. Sometimes in this situation, parents just give up—what's the use?

This reaction is not uncommon, but your children will count on you to be strong—to still be their parent. So, keep spending time with them. Keep doing everything you can to participate in their lives. It may not be the situation you would have chosen, but your children must be able to count on you. You are their guide—you are their protector and defender.

Do not abandon your children—not even for a moment. Do not threaten to leave them. It is imperative that they absolutely and unquestionably know, especially in times of crisis, that you will always be there for them, even if you live in a separate place.

5. Sign-up for Joint Counseling—By Yourself!!

Some co-parents believe that they have nothing to learn from counseling, and they refuse to go. That shouldn't discourage you. Just go by yourself.

Years ago, I got a call from a friend who asked for the name of a marriage counselor for her son and daughter-in-law. I gave her the name of a psychologist in the area, and she said, "Oh, my gosh! You just gave me the name of the person who saved my marriage!"

She went on to explain that she and her husband needed to go to marriage counseling, but he refused. So, she went by herself. She described her husband and her situation to the therapist, and he taught her how to work effectively with him.

So, if you can't get the other parent to go to counseling, go by yourself and explain your situation to the therapist. Describe your co-parent and ask the counselor to teach you how to work with that person. It can be extremely helpful.

6. Change the Story

Divorce is not a failure; it can be the greatest opportunity of your life

You may feel miserable as you read this, and you may be tempted to blame your co-parent, your family or the outside world.

It may sound corny, but divorce is, in fact, a new beginning. It is a new path—a path on which you will create a better life for yourself—physically (diet and exercise), mentally (therapy, classes, new educational goals) and spiritually (new thoughts, new ideas).

You'll know when you are ready. Seize the moment, and let go of habits that don't serve you.

7. Stand Up Straight—Be an Alpha Parent

Be strong

There are times when you will feel weak and exhausted. And, in case you haven't noticed, your kids can smell weakness. They may seize the opportunity to misbehave and show you just how rude they can really be.

Solution? Take a deep breath, stand up tall, spread your arms and take control. Assume the Wonder Woman or Superman stance. Your kids will back down, and you will feel stronger!

8. Be Grateful

Practice gratitude to change your attitude

Count your blessings each day. At the very least, it will make you happier. Some researchers believe that being grateful reduces depression. It changes the way you look at things.

So, find something (or many things) for which to be grateful.

What has gone well for you this week?

Is the sun shining?

Did you get any good news?

Even if you can find only the tiniest thing, be appreciative. It will change your attitude. It may make your life easier. And it will set a good example for your children.

9. Smile

Feeling down? Try smiling

If you feel down, try smiling.

Smile at everyone you meet. You'll be surprised—you will discover that is has a cyclical effect. People will smile back, and that will make you feel better. And soon, your smile will become real, and you will notice that you are much happier. Everyone is drawn to positive people. So ... keep smiling and enjoy the reactions of others. It works with your kids too.

10. Be Kind

Like a smile, kindness begets kindness. It's amazing. It's even contagious. The more you give, the more you receive. Your children will learn from watching you.

11. Eat Right, Exercise and Breathe

This is all about you and your health, not just your mental and economic health, but your physical health as well. Divorce is hard—physically, emotionally and spiritually. You must take extra care to eat properly, exercise regularly and breathe deeply. Can't hurt, and it may help—a lot.

12. Use Your Head and Your Heart

Think with both your head and your heart.

Your divorce will tax your brain. There will be forms to fill out, a household to divide, daily chores to maintain and tasks to just survive. It's a load. So, engage your heart as well as your head and remember the loving person you know you can be. Let love pour out, even if you aren't feeling very loving. Your heart will support you and will give you strength. Just put your hand on your heart, close your eyes and enjoy the quiet. Think thoughts of love and peace. You will find a new way to relax and clear your cluttered brain.

13. Treat Your Co-Parent with Respect ... Even if You Have Been Betrayed

This is a hard one.

Perhaps the other parent has betrayed you or hurt you or disappointed you. And you still have to be respectful?

Yes—for the sake of your children. He or she is their parent, and that will never change. You allow them to continue to love the other parent by showing respect. It's not so much for the benefit of the other parent. It's for the mental health of your children and for their resiliency. It will also help you let go of a lot of negative emotional junk. It's not easy, but it is likely (not guaranteed) to pay off in the long run.

14. Attend the Neighborhood BBQ

Bring the baked beans, but don't bring the divorce

You're newly separated or in the middle of an angry divorce, and you and your co-parent are invited to a neighborhood BBQ. Your kids are excited. This has been a family tradition for many years. They want you both to attend … and you should.

But how can you stand next to the person who has hurt you? Here's the answer: buckle up, buttercup. Put a smile on your face, and make it through the event. When things get edgy, walk away and join a new conversation. Don't discuss the divorce. Stand tall. Each time you do this, you will improve your ability to cope, and it will become easier. The message to the children is that you can all join the party or the celebration because you, their parents, are committed to them and you love them. You will successfully keep the conflict away from them. Congratulations!

15. Stay Ahead of Life

Think to the future

One of the best things that you can do for yourself and your children is to plan ahead.

Try to think of the things that you want to do with your life.

Take a look at your finances. What will you need to do to stay ahead of any financial crises?

Do you need to go back to school? Can you make that happen?

What about your children's needs?

When do you do school shopping?

Will one of the kids need braces? I

It's a really good idea to do an individual plan (as well as the Family Commitment Statement), so you can see where you want to go and how you will get there.

16. Save Money

Take a deep breath

There's nothing like having a little nest egg that is all yours.

Start by setting aside money before you pay any bills. Deposit it in a separate account or have an automatic deposit made to two accounts—one would be your little rat hole and one for paying the bills. You might use it to pay for an emergency or a car or a vacation. But it will be yours—set aside and ready to go! Financial security eases the household pressure and allows everybody to relax a bit. It reduces your anxiety and that trickles down to the kids. Less anxiety? More time to develop resilience.

17. Bring Color into Your Life

Lift your spirits (and those of your children)

Color can make such a difference when you are going through tough times. How about painting a room yellow or bright blue? Paint is relatively inexpensive, and it will make a big difference. You might want to stay away from red—it is a powerful and sometimes insightful color. Blue is soothing, yellow will lift your spirits, green denotes harmony, and violet is considered to be spiritual. If nothing else, a fresh coat of paint will reflect a fresh start to your life. The kids can participate—let them choose a paint color for their bedrooms. They, too, are starting a new phase of their lives, and you want them to be strong, creative and resilient.

18. Commit/Recommit/Reflect/Release/Recommit

The parenting road after divorce is not an easy one—but it can be a good one. Always be aware of where you are emotionally, physically and financially. Always be aware of how your children are doing. If, after reflection, you need to go back to the drawing board, don't hesitate. Very few situations are irretrievable. Take a deep breath. Recommit. Reflect on you new direction. Release the old junk. Now, recommit again. You will make it.

9

Reach Out
to the Community

Americans spend approximately $36 **Billion** per year on their divorces.[xxxviii] Just recently, I was told of a divorce that cost the parties over $500,000 in legal and professional fees. That's a lot of anger! Who has that kind of money to kiss off—and who would want to do it?

Divorce also affects the workplace and costs employers millions of dollars each year.[xxxix] It is the cause of increased absenteeism, tardiness, on-the-job injuries, property damage, medical claims, decreased attention to the job, burnout, mental health problems and diminished job performance, among other things.

However, the enormous financial cost associated with divorce is miniscule compared with the damage that can be done to the children of divorce. This is a public health crisis that must be addressed on an individual level, on a community level and on a national level. So, what can you do?

1. Keep a Watchful Eye

Watch for children and adults who are in pain.

You can read a child from a block away—and you can read his mom or dad. Are they sad? Do they seem lost? They may be victims of toxic stress and absolutely unable to fend for themselves.

I watched this happen on my grandson's soccer team. One of the players was a young boy from Ethiopia named Aaron. When he was adopted and came to this country, he couldn't speak English. He was totally unfamiliar with anything about his new surroundings—except soccer. All you needed to play soccer in Ethiopia was a ball, and he had played constantly in the orphanage that had been his home.

Aaron learned English quickly and made a remarkable adjustment to his new home. He was a star athlete who made friends easily. He seemed to be thriving.

Unfortunately, his adoptive mom subsequently got divorced. It was a nasty divorce that was filled with acrimony. The shouting and verbal abuse in the home was intense. Aaron's mother quickly turned her attention to finding a new husband and ignored Aaron and his brother.

Aaron began to flounder. His grades fell, and he started getting into trouble. He was being humiliated by his older brother and was alienated from his adoptive father. He felt no support from his mother and was left to drift into trouble on a path previously forged by his brother.

The wife of the soccer coach, Jan, noticed the difference in Aaron, and began to help him. He spent a lot of time at their house. She insisted that he (and her son) do their home-work, treat their friends and other adults with respect and get exercise. She taught him basic hygiene, took him to get haircuts and helped him in other ways.

Aaron's mother was really pleased because she didn't have to take the time to help him. Jan literally saved his life. She took him from an environment filled with toxic stress and taught him resilience.

We can each make a difference in our community. Be alert. Watch for children who look like they need some support. Reach out to the family. You can make a huge impact in a child's life.

2. Form a Neighborhood Group

You look like s__t. What's the matter with you?

There are lots of reasons for people to get together, but whatever the reason, it's the sense of community and friendship that is important. For people who are going through a divorce and their children, it could be a life saver.

Several days after my first husband announced that he wanted a divorce and moved out of our house, I was dropping our younger child off at preschool. One of the other mothers whom I had met, but whom I did not really know ("Mitzi"), came up to me and said, "You look like s__t, what's the matter with you?" I predictably burst into tears and explained to her that my husband had just moved out, and it looked like we were going to get a divorce.

Without hesitation, Mitzi took me in—literally and figuratively. We became best friends and formed a coffee group of women in the neighborhood. She stood by me in some very dark hours and helped me maintain my sanity and keep the divorce issues away from my kids. She stands as a bright star who had the nerve to reach out and bring me to a place of healing.

Our coffee group met regularly and supported local school and community events. We watched out for the neighborhood children and made certain that they were each accounted for and were safe. We provided the kind of help that supports resiliency in the children—they knew we were there for them. You don't need too many best friends. But having a few friends whom you trust is critical.

It's a good lesson. Don't be afraid to reach out. Don't be afraid to offer support.

3. Maintain Safe Environments

How often do you hear of someone who gets fired and then comes back to the workplace with a gun? It's scary. And, while it appears to be unpredictable, it probably is very predictable.

Everyone should be on the watch for people who are overly stressed or acting erratically. While you don't want to put yourself in danger, you might want to speak to someone in authority if you are at all suspicious. Safety in the community is critical to a sense of well-being for all citizens—especially children.

4. Support Your Schools

Good schools are the foundation of our country, and there are many ways that you can support them

Good schools produce good students. However, good schools don't just happen. They require the support of the faculty, the administration and (especially) the parents. Here's some things you can do for your school and your kids:

- *Help out in the classroom.* Get to know your children's teachers. Make sure that the teachers understand your situation and how important it is for your children to gain confidence and resilience.

- *Form a school district foundation.* Many school districts have foundations that raise money for classroom teachers. In Olympia, Washington, for example, the Olympia School District Education Foundation raises money for the Principal's Emergency Checkbook Fund, an outdoor fifth grade education program, grants and an art's initiative. None of these programs would exist without the foundation. The money that they raise goes to kids who otherwise couldn't afford to participate in these activities.

- *Support alternative school programs.* Many school districts are forming innovative programs that provide alternative school environments for the students and benefit the community. One such program is the Freedom Farmers at Muirhead Farm program, in which disengaged and/or low income students grow 50% of the produce for the Olympia, WA school district and the community. They focus on the themes of Farming Self (personal development), Farming Land (sustainable land stewardship), and Farming Community (civic engagement and community service). It is a successful alternative that can reach young people who, for a variety of reasons, have become separated from their school community. It brightens their lives and lets them know that people in the community care about them.

Reach out to your school district. What can you do to help children who are suffering from one or more ACEs? It is a way to give back.

5. Speak up at Work

Ask any employer.

Do employees who are going through a divorce work at their highest capacity?

The answer is "no."

They are usually exhausted, scared, preoccupied, short-tempered, and late or absent due to court appearances. This doesn't even touch on the effects of domestic violence, mental health problems, addiction, alcoholism and medical claims.

Does this cost the employer money?

Yes, it does.

Many businesses today have employee assistance programs (EAPs) that provide education, counseling, referrals and other services. EAPs, however, are often not available in small companies.

As an employee, you might consider working with your Human Resources Department or your EAP to make sure that the services that are being offered are effective. Education classes can be very helpful, especially if the message is repeated again and again: Conflict hurts every family member, but it especially hurts kids. Employers and employees must work together to find a way to resolve conflict. It will benefit the employer's bottom line. It will benefit the employee. It will benefit everybody.

6. Change the Rules—Change the Statutes

We have been approaching divorce all wrong

Our court system is not designed to solve family issues. As William Howe, a highly respected family law attorney from Oregon stated:

> *Adversarial proceedings discourage cooperation, too often regard aggressive posturing and positional bargaining, and sabotage the ability of the parents to work together as child-rearing partners. In short, the adversarial model fuels parental conflict, and parental conflict over children is universally understood to be harmful to the children.*[xl]

Courts and professional organizations are responding to the problem. Organizations such as the Institute for the Advancement of the American Legal System (IAALS), the American Bar Association (ABA) and the Association of Family and Conciliation Courts (AFCC) are working with lawyers, legal scholars, mental health professionals and legislators to develop practical ideas to improve the delivery of legal services and access to justice. Judges are creating self-help offices that are staffed with people who can provide guidance to divorcing parties. And couples are using mediation, collaborative law and arbitration as ways to stay out of court. But, in addition to all that has been done, we need to change the rules.

On December 1, 2016, the Colorado Supreme Court approved an Amendment to Comment [2] of Rule 2.1 of the Colorado Rules of Professional Conduct that govern attorneys in the state. The amendment provides:

> *In a matter involving the allocation of parental rights and responsibilities, a lawyer should consider advising the client that parental conflict can have a significant adverse effect on minor children.*

Colorado is the first state in the country to adopt an Amendment to their Rules concerning children.

The objective of the amendment is to bring attention to the fact that children are being harmed by their parents' unresolved conflict, and lawyers (who have a duty to their client) should consider discussing the issue with their client. It is but one example of the way in which people can start to change the legal system, so that it becomes more focused on children.

You can make such changes in your state. If you can't change the professional rules, you might talk to your legislators about amending your state statutes.

You may also want to lobby for the ratification by the United States of the United Nations Convention on the Rights of the Child (the UNCRC or the Convention). This is a human rights treaty which sets out the civil, political, economic, social, health and cultural rights of children. Nations that ratify the UNCRC are bound to it by international law. Governments of countries that have ratified it are required to report to, and appear before, the United Nations Committee on the Rights of the Child and to be examined on their progress regarding the advancement of the implementation of the Convention and the status of child rights in their country. To date, 196 countries are party to the Convention, including every member of the United Nations **EXCEPT** the United States. A simple letter to Nikki Haley, the United States Ambassador to the United Nations, could begin a campaign that would be heard.

Remember—you can make a difference.

7. Change the National Conversation

For years, we have assumed that judges can correct everything in the family. It comes as a surprise to some people, who have to go to trial in order to get their divorce, that the court really can't make everything okay. In fact, the judge's rulings, while consistent with the law, may make everything worse.

We have been approaching divorce all wrong. Instead of asking a judge to decide what is best for the children, you, as parents, must answer that question before going to court. You must take back your authority and decide the fate of your children. And we need to shout this message from the rooftops!

This is the start of a grassroots campaign to promote the well-being of children in the divorce process. When parents take the responsibility, they will save money, time and stress. They will allow their children to be free to be kids— not little adults who are scared or who have to take care of their parents. It is time to focus on the success and happiness of the children.

A name for this movement?

How about *responsible parents/resilient kids.com*?

Speak Out! The message is clear: Conflict Hurts Kids and It Is Not Acceptable.

10

Making It Easy— Follow the Six C's

Conflict can start anytime and anyplace, but it is usually a waste of time, energy and often money. So, before you start or join into a fight, think about your children and decide if this is worth it.

Parental conflict starts and stops with you. Consider the 6C's—It's an easy summary:

- **COMMIT** to your children. Actually, take it one step further, make a commitment to your family. It will still exist after you are divorced, and it is the first family for your children. We call it the Post-Divorce Family.

  Put your kids and your Post-Divorce Family at the front of your mind. Some people will actually touch their forehead and consciously consider what the children would think about the fight in which they are about to start or join. More often than not, it is enough to slow things down and move in a different direction. You are a KEY influencer in the process and in the outcome. Choose happiness and harmony for you and your kids. The alternative is sadness and dysfunction. It's a no-brainer—right?

- **COMPARTMENTALIZE** your anger. Separate your anger with the other parent from your relationship with the kids. Don't discuss the intimate details of your divorce with your children or criticize the other parent in their presence.

  Many people use compartmentalization as a technique for problem-solving. It allows you to step away from the immediate issue and control your emotions and communication. It also allows you to find space in your brain and heart to find ways to solve the immediate problem. Most importantly, it takes the conflict away from the children.

- **COMMUNICATE** with the other parent about kid issues. Talk. Even though you may find it distasteful or painful, don't give up. Your kids need you to be the parent. However, there are guidelines that you should consider:

  First, make sure your messages are TRUTHFUL, NECESSARY AND KIND. These three principles will guide you through the most difficult of situations.

Second, think about your message before you push "send" or confront the other parent. Messages sent in haste often reflect the emotion you are experiencing at the moment and may not be accurate. Think before you send or confront. Unless it's an emergency or time sensitive, most information can wait to be conveyed.

Third, figure out a way to communicate. If you really have difficulty speaking with the other parent, you may want to use an interactive computer program to email or text messages. Always remember to speak respectfully and to avoid demeaning the other parent.

Fourth, some people take post-divorce communication classes. You will need to communicate about kid issues for most of the rest of your life. So, you might as well learn early on how to do it well. Talk. Even though it may be difficult, don't give up.

- **CONSIDER** the ideas of your children. They will not make the final decisions—that's a job for you and the other parent. But your kids need to know that you will listen to them. Children are stakeholders in the family. They have ideas and concerns. They do not want to be ignored or shuttled aside. Listening to them is one way to let them know that they are important and loved.

- **CHANGE** your approach to conflict. Remember the key theme of this book: Conflict hurts kids. So, your challenge is to change the way you deal with conflict and keep it away from the kids.

There are many ways you can do this. First, it starts with you. Practice avoiding the fight by acknowledging the other person's concerns and clearly stating your concerns. Treat the other parent with respect and try a little humor. Watch your body language ... crossing your arms, pointing your finger, refusing to make eye contact ... these are signals that you do not want to communicate.

And, if necessary, take a high-conflict class. You can find someone to help you by Googling "high conflict classes" or try using search terms such as: "parenting conflict classes" or "conflict during divorce classes." It is really worth it to get some help. Remember, in addition to saving you time and money, you are really saving the lives of your children.

- **CALL 911** if you or your children are in imminent danger. There are times when the conflict between you and the other parent becomes dangerous. Although it is amazingly unfortunate for children to witness police coming to their home, it is sometimes necessary to protect yourself and them. If there is imminent danger, don't hesitate. MAKE THE CALL!

A Final Thought

I am always amazed at the power of thought. I have contemplated writing this book for several years. My friends, to be truthful, had gotten a little tired of hearing about it. My problem, however, was that I didn't think I had anything to add to what I had already written in my last book, *Parenting Plans for Families After Divorce.*

Then, quite serendipitously, I started meeting people from the Kempe Center for the Prevention and Treatment of Child Abuse and Neglect, a remarkable resource in Denver, Colorado. First I met Ren Cannon, who is the co-chairman of the Kempe Ambassadors. He steered me to Jon Faught, the president and CEO of the Kempe Foundation, and then to Desmond K. Runyan, MD, PhD, the executive director of the Kempe Center. They introduced me to the ACEs Study. I am very grateful to them—thank you.

After I researched ACEs and Dr. Runyan's work on the LONGSCAN Study, I discussed this information with friends who practice in the area of family law. I had not heard of it, and neither had most of them. It obviously involves information that needs to be given to parents and lawyers, and it formed the foundation for this book.

It is my hope that the legal community can catch up with the pediatric community and spread the word: Unresolved conflict hurts kids. I am very optimistic that we can convey the message and change the paradigm of divorce.

Acknowledgments

There are many people who have stood by me and helped me write this book. My two daughters and their families are first on the list. They are amazing and truly the gifts of my life. I am also grateful to the rest of my family—how fortunate I am to be surrounded by supportive people whom I love.

I have great friends who must be acknowledged. Their help has been remarkable. This would include Gina Weitzenkorn, Helen Shreves, Diana Powell, Ann Gushurst, Hon. Angela Arkin (ret.), David Littman, and Sue Waters. They each supported the Amendment to the Colorado Rules of Professional Conduct and testified before the Standing Committee of the Colorado Supreme Court. Bob Hinds, Rob Hinds, Dr. Les Katz, Alec Rothrock and Hon. Cheryl Post (ret.) were part of the original committee. Marcie Glenn, the chairperson of the Colorado Supreme Court Standing Committee, and Alec Rothrock, also a member of the Standing Committee, were particularly helpful. My appreciation goes to the rest of the Standing Committee for their support as well as to the Justices on the Colorado Supreme Court who unanimously approved the amendment.

I also wish to thank the Executive Council of the Family Law Section of the Colorado Bar Association. Members of the council were the first to approve the amendment, and they supported printing 20,000 flyers on parental conflict to hand out to family law attorneys, judges, court facilitators, sherlocks, and mental health professionals for their clients.

My sincere thanks to Hon. Rebecca Kourlis, the executive director of the University of Denver Institute for the Advancement of the American Legal System. She has been a great help to me and has made an invaluable contribution to the legal system and to the practice of law through her work.

I have had many other friends who have listened to me and have given me their tireless support! This includes Cindy Halaby, Melinda Douglas, Pam Gagel, Melinda Taylor, Autumn Miller, Kate McNamara, the Hon. Elizabeth Stroebel, the Yoga girls and the Green Diamonds.

I am also most appreciative for the help I received from the Kempe Center for the Prevention and Treatment of Child Abuse and Neglect—in particular—Ren Cannon, John Faught and Dr. Desmond Runyan. They gave me direction at a time when I particularly needed it. Special thanks also to Lori Jackson, the executive director of the National Foundation to End Child Abuse and Neglect; she is an inspiration.

I am particularly grateful to Jack Harding, a lawyer in Denver who completed the initial edit of the book and did a fabulous job. The Hon. Rebecca Kourlis, Sue Caparelli, Pam Gagel, Bonnie Schriner, Sheila Gutterman, and Mike Daniels edited the book and made enormous contributions. Jen Zelinger did the line edits, and Nick Zelinger (NZ Graphics) designed the cover and completed the layout. Kelly Johnson of Virtual Assistance, LLC, played a key role in helping me with the IT side of publishing. A special shout out to Mike Daniels, publisher coach, who came up with the name of the book and offered many suggestions—great job! And ... loving thanks again to my daughters, Jeanette and Kendall, who have been at my side every step of the way.

Thank you all.

Finally, I am extremely grateful to you, the readers. I hope this book will make a difference in the lives of your children.

Thank you.
Joan McWilliams

About the Author

Joan McWilliams is a pioneer in the field of mediation. Before starting her mediation practice more than thirty years ago, she served as a law clerk for the 10th Circuit Court of Appeals and subsequently became a partner in a large Denver law firm.

Joan has been an active member of the Colorado Bar Association and was a co-initiator of the Colorado Parental Responsibilities Act. She is the recipient of the Alumni Professional Award from the University Of Denver Sturm College Of Law and the Family Law Icon Award from the Colorado Bar Association.

In 2017, Joan devoted a year to creating a proposal to amend a Comment to the Colorado Rules of Professional Conduct that states that lawyers should consider advising separating and divorcing clients that parental conflict can have significant adverse effects on their children. On December 1, 2017, the Colorado Supreme Court unanimously approved the proposed amendment, making Colorado the first state in the country to approve such a provision.

First listed with *Best Lawyers* in 2005, Joan has been honored as a "Lawyer of the Year" twice in family law mediation. She was recognized by *Super Lawyers* and as *Law Week Colorado's 2016 Barrister's Best Mediator* and *2017 People's Choice Best Mediator*. She was named as *2012 and*

2017 Best Lawyers Lawyer of the Year—Family Law Mediation and the *2018 Arbitration Lawyer of the Year.* Joan was also awarded the *2016 Richard N. Doyle CLE Award of Excellence.* She has written two books: *Parenting Plans for Families after Divorce* and the award-winning book, *The PeaceFinder: Riley McFee's Quest for World Peace.*

Joan continues to actively practice divorce mediation and is available for speaking engagements. She may be contacted at (303)830-0171 or *joan@mcwilliamsmediation.com.*

Endnotes

[i] Rebecca Love Kourlis, *It is Just Good Business: The Case For Supporting Reform In Divorce Court*, 50 Family Court Review 4 (2012) 549-557 citing Paul R. Amato, *The Consequences of Divorce for Adults and Children*, 62 J. MARRIAGE & FAM. (2000) 1269.

[ii] Vincent J. Felitti, MD and Robert F. Anda, MD, MS, *Chapter 10: Lifelong Effects of Adverse Childhood Experiences*, Vol 2, Fourth Edition, Chadwick's Child Maltreatment (STM Learning, Inc.) 203-216.

[iii] Martin H. Teicher, M.D., PhD et al, *Sticks, Stones, and Hurtful Words: Relative Effects of Various Forms of Childhood Maltreatment*, 163 American Journal of Psychiatry (2006) 993.

[iv] Erv Hinds, MD, *Healing the Pain of Heartache: A Physician Explores Broken Heart Syndrome*, (2010) 9. See also https://video.com/88806942.

[v] Carol Gerwin, Toxic Stress, Center on the Developing Child at Harvard University (2013) 1.

[vi] *Id.*

[vii] *Id. at 2.*

[viii] *Id.*

[ix] Hon. Beth Dumler conducted an informal study of the juveniles that appeared before her when she was a Magistrate in Douglas County, Colorado. She found that 80% of the juveniles experienced their parent's high conflict divorce or were abandoned.

[x] *See* Sol R. Rappaport, *Deconstructing the Impact of Divorce on Children*, 47 Family Law Quarterly 3(Fall 2013) 351.

[xi] *Supra* at note ii, Chapter 10: *Lifelong Effects of Adverse Childhood Experiences.*

[xii] David Fijkelhor, PhD et al, *Improving the Adverse Childhood Experiences Study Scale*, 167(1) *JAMA Pediatr* (2013) 70-75.

[xiii] *Id.*

[xiv] Nadine Burke Harris, M.D., *The Deepest Well: Healing the Long-Term Effects of Childhood Adversity*, Houghton Mifflin Harcourt (Boston 2018) 59.

[xv] Sarah Watamura and Samantha Brown, *Parental History of Adversity and Child Well-being: Insights from Colorado*, Colorado Office of Early Childhood, Department of Human Services (May 2017).

[xvi] Ziba Kashef, *Toxic Stress Exposure in Childhood Linked to Risky Behavior, Adult Disease*, Yale News (November 19, 2015).

[xvii] Center for Disease Control and Prevention, *Quick Stats: Suicide Rates for Teens Aged 15-19 Years by Sex—United States, 1975-2015* (August 4, 2017).

[xviii] *Id.*

[xix] *Supra* at note iii, *Sticks, Stones, and Hurtful Words: Relative Effects of Various Forms of Childhood Maltreatment.*

[xx] *Id.*

xxi R. Douglas Fields Ph.D., *The New Brain*, Psychology Today (Oct 30, 2010).

xxii *Id.*

xxiii Claudine Black, M.S.W., Ph.D., *Understanding the Pain of Abandonment*, Psychology Today (Posted June 4, 2010).

xxiv Jenna Rowen and Robert Emery, *Parental Denigration: A Form of Conflict That Typically Backfires*, 56 Family Court Review 2 (April 2018) 258.

xxv *Id.*

xxvi *Id.* at 267.

xxvii *Supra* at note iv, *Healing the Pain of Heartache: A Physician Explores Broken Heart Syndrome.*

xxviii *Id.*

xxix *Id.* at 50.

xxx Printed with permission from Dr. Desmond Runyan, the Executive Director of The Kempe Center for the Prevention and Treatment of Child Abuse and Neglect and a Professor of Pediatrics at the University of Colorado. Dr. Runyan was a Principal Investigator for the LONGSCAN study ("Longitudinal Studies of Child Abuse and Neglect").

xxxi J.D. Vance, *Hillbilly Elegy: A Memoir of a Family and Culture in Crisis*, Harper Collins (2016) 253, 254-255.

xxxii Joan H. McWilliams, *Parenting Plans for Families After Divorce*, McWilliams Mediation Group LTD, (2011).

[xxxiii] National Center for Trauma-Informed Care & Alternatives to Seclusion and Restraint, www.samhsa.gov/nctic/trauma-interventions

[xxxiv] Printed with permission from Lori Jackson, MA, LPC, RRT, Executive Director of the National Foundation to End Child Abuse and Neglect.

[xxxv] *Id.*

[xxxvi] Women's Charter, Part X, Section 94A.

[xxxvii] In some counties in the country, sheriff's deputies and police officers use the Lethality Assessment Program when they are sent on domestic violence calls. They ask victims questions that are intended to screen for domestic violence. If the victim gives "yes" answers, the officer contacts the nearest Crisis Center to determine the next step. This process has been effective because it gives officers a way to ask difficult questions, and it allows victims to express how serious their situation is.

[xxxviii] *Supra* at note i, *It is Just Good Business: The Case For Supporting Reform In Divorce Court.*

[xxxix] *Id.*

[xl] William J. Howe and Hugh McIsaac, *Finding the Balance: Ethical Challenges and Best Practices for Lawyers Representing Parents When the Interests of the Children are at Stake,* 46 Family Court Review 1 (January 2008) 78-90.